Bronllys Castle

THE CASTLES OF MID WALES
Mike Salter

CONTENTS

INTRODUCTION

The type of defensible lordly residence which the Normans called a castle was unknown in Wales until the Normans invaded the country in the 11th century. They had evolved a class of building usually having a stone or timber tower acting as both a citadel and as a secure dwelling for the owner. Such citadels were not found in the forts built by Welsh princes and chieftains hitherto, nor in the forts constructed by the Romans. Norman courtiers of the penultimate Saxon King of England, Edward the Confessor, built three castles in Herefordshire in the 1050s and after the invasion of England in 1066 they were built in profusion throughout the country, proving an effective means of keeping the Saxons subjugated. The Normans also created a system whereby great lords held land from the King in return for military service and they in turn let knights hold land from them in return for specified periods of military service annually, which often took the form of garrison duty at a castle.

The early Norman Kings of England attempted to create a barrier against the Welsh by creating marcher lordships whose holders were allowed to have more compact groups of manors than elsewhere which resulted in greater military strength, and, having their own courts, they became effectively petty kings themselves. Before long these lords became dangerous occasional competitors to the English Crown but it was not until 1536 that it was possible to officially abolish them. Shropshire and Herefordshire then assumed their present shape whilst the counties of Brecon (formerly called Brecknock), Radnor, and Montgomery forming the subject of this book, and which in 1974 were officially united as the county of Powys, were newly created.

William the Conqueror and his successor William Rufus allowed the Marcher lords to make whatever progress they could in occupying Wales which was then ruled by three princes of Gwynedd, Deheubarth, and Powys, plus a number of lesser independent rulers. Welsh custom divided property equally among all sons and allowed any adult male close relative to claim the title of a deceased ruler and this led to perpetual family squabbles and military and economic weakness which the Normans were able to exploit. Roger de Montgomery, named after Montgomerie in Normandy, built a castle then called Montgomery but now known as Hen Domen in the 1070s. Two other castles in the Severn valley are likely to be relics of his advances in the 1080s.

In 1093 the Normans made a major breakthrough when Bernard de Newmarch defeated and killed Rhys ap Tewdwr, ruler of Deheubarth, and captured Gwrgan ap Bleddyn, ruler of Brycheiniog, in a battle near Brecon where Bernard then built a castle. His followers built chains of castles along the river valleys, notably Aberllynfi, Hay, and Bronllys beside the Wye, and Pencelli, Tretower, and Crickhowell along the Usk. Ralph Mortimer advanced from Wigmore Castle to take Elfael and Maelienydd from the Welsh. He or his followers built the castles of Radnor, Knighton, Gemaron, and Cefnllys. Shortly after Pain Fitz-John built the castle named after him in Radnorshire and Philip de Braose created a lordship based on Builth Castle.

The Welsh hotly contested the Norman territorial gains. In 1094 Roger de Newburgh had to rescue Bernard de Newmarch from a state of semi-siege at Brecon. That castle held out against the Welsh on several occasions, except perhaps in the 1260s. However, the other castles such as Builth, Gemaron, and Cefnllys, were over the next two centuries repeatedly captured and destroyed by the Welsh when they temporarily united under strong leaders and the English were weak (like during the anarchy in England of 1136-54), only to be rebuilt when the Normans recovered their strength. Eventually the Welsh, especially the often pro-Norman rulers of Powys, began to build castles themselves such as that at Welshpool erected in 1111.

Cilwybert Motte

Dolbedwyn Motte

The first castle site at Cefnllys

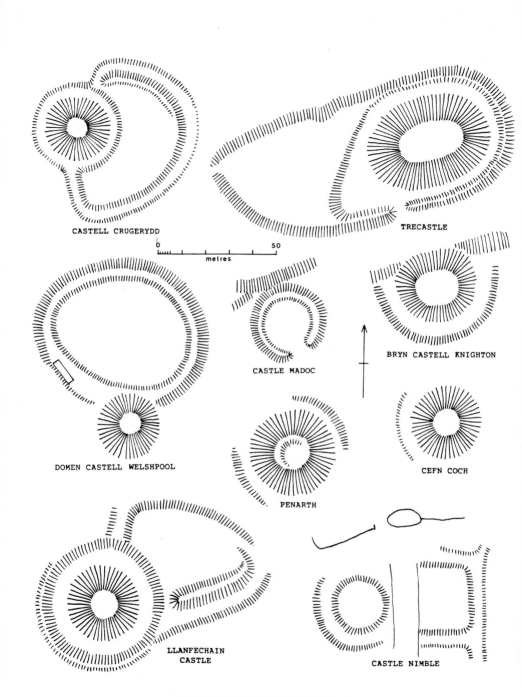

CASTELL CRUGERYDD

TRECASTLE

0   50
metres

CASTLE MADOC

BRYN CASTELL KNIGHTON

DOMEN CASTELL WELSHPOOL

CEFN COCH

PENARTH

LLANFECHAIN
CASTLE

CASTLE NIMBLE

PLANS OF CASTLE EARTHWORKS

None of these early castles in Mid-Wales were stone buildings. They were built of earth and wood which required less craftsmen and were more suitable materials for cheap and quick construction work by gangs of slave labour. A common form comprised an earth mound or motte surmounted by a timber tower with a small palisaded courtyard around it, with a bailey or larger court at the base containing a hall, chapel, workshops, stables, granary and other farm buildings constructed of wood, wattle-and-daub, or unmortared stone within a rampart and ditch. The tower on the mound formed a private dwelling for the lord and a last refuge if the weaker bailey defences should succumb to an attack. The basic design was varied according to the terrain, labour, and time available. A small enclosure with a high bank (known to castle enthusiasts as a ringwork) might replace the motte, whilst baileys were omitted or duplicated or laid out to whatever shape and size the terrain suggested. An outer bank often lay beyond the main ditch and sometimes another ditch beyond that. Natural spurs and hillocks were utilised where possible, being made into steep-sided, level-topped mottes. The remains survive of over 100 earthworks of this type created in Mid Wales by the year 1200, good specimens being at Builth, Hen Domen, Llanfechain, Gro Tump, Rhos Ddiarbed, Pain's Castle and Trecastle.

Stone blocks were occasionally used as the cores of mottes and small buildings were sometimes crudely built of unmortared stone but proper masonry walls required capital, numerous craftsmen, and fairly peaceful conditions for several years for their construction. In the area covered by this book the earliest surviving masonry is the shell wall of c1160 at Tretower. Norman windows survive in the parts of the shell which had two storey blocks containing a solar or private room and a hall, and there was also a small square tower to contain the gateway. Probably the more important castle at Brecon gained its shell keep at about the same time. Other shell walls at Symon's Castle and Crickhowell may be later. The substantial square tower keep at Pencelli, and the smaller square towers at Bleddfa, Hyssington, and Hay may have existed by the 1190s. These buildings would contain a cellar at ground level reached only by a trap-door from the hall or main living room reached by a timber stair from the ground, and then a bedroom on top. A typical Late Norman window survives at Hay where the inner arch of the gateway is not likely to be much later. At Castell Dinas are footings of a rectangular keep probably only originally two storeys high with a low chemise wall around it, a modest inner ward with square towers adjoining, and a larger outer ward. The only dateable feature is later than c1200 but the keep, chemise, and inner ward may be of c1180-1200. The only historical record of the period likely to concern masonry construction at any of the castles refers to the now vanished wall built around the bailey at Carreghofa in 1194.

The building of a new stone castle at Montgomery by Henry III in the 1220s to replace Hen Domen heralded a spate of replacements of timber defences by stone walls. The new castle had a small but strong inner ward with a large D-shaped tower on one side and was entered through a gatehouse containing the main hall and chamber, and which was fronted by two round towers. In the 1230s Henry III built a curtain wall with towers and a gatehouse and a round tower keep on the motte at Pain's Castle and he repaired recent damage done to Hay Castle. At the same time the Picards built a round keep and curtain walls with towers at Tretower and the Cliffords did the same at Bronllys. In the 1240s Henry III rebuilt Builth Castle and walled in the middle ward at Montgomery whilst the Mortimer family built a new castle at Cefnllys and strengthened Blaenllynfi. It may have been about the same time that a curtain wall with a gatehouse was built at Brecon by the Bohun family.

Montgomery Castle

Tretower
Castle

Thomas Corbet began building a square court with corner towers on the rock now known as Nantcribba in the 1260s but Llywelyn ap Gruffudd took advantage of the civil war in England at that period to capture and destroy many of the Mortimer castles in Maelienydd and Elfael, and to occupy the district around the de Bohun seat at Brecon so more was demolished than was erected. The Welsh probably built the small pentagonal court at Castell Coch with a rectangular keep and one large round tower in the 1260s, and in the early 1270s Llywelyn himself built an oblong court with the same two elements at either end at Dolforwyn to assert his authority in Powys and defy the English Crown. The Mortimers refortified Cefnllys, Tinboeth, and Pencelli in the 1270s whilst the Bohuns built a large isolated round keep at Blaencamlais. Cefnllys also has a keep, either round or octagonal, within a modest square court with round corner towers. Tinboeth was oval without flanking towers although there was a big gatehouse which may have been twin-round-towered like that which is known to have stood at Pencelli until the 18th century.

Edward I carried out some remodelling at Montgomery and in 1277 began rebuilding Builth Castle with a round keep and a curtain with six D-shaped towers and a gatehouse as part of his campaign against Llywelyn ap Gruffudd. The works were left unfinished after Llywelyn was killed in a skirmish nearby in 1282. No-one else was able to unite the Welsh and the need for strong new fortfications lessened although in the 1280s Mortimer supporters rebuilt Crickhowell Castle and erected a new castle at Aberedw which was square with circular corner towers. In c1300 the Bohuns built a new hall block at Brecon which is now the only domestic building surviving in a recognisable state in any of the castles. The very ruined mid 14th century works at Llanddew are not very military in character and the only other buildings of note are at Powis where the former princes appear to have built a square keep and separate hall block in c1280-1300 to which their successors the Charltons added a massive pair of drum towers either side of the inner gate and an outer ward with further round towers in the first half of the 14th century. Of about the same period are the mysterious and somewhat altered tower houses at Scethrog and Talgarth which seem to have lacked courtyards.

6

There is both documentary and archeological evidence of timber buildings on motte and bailey castles being maintained until c1300 and occasionally beyond. The pudding-bowl shaped mottes all seem to be of c1175-1185 but other earthwork types were sometimes built in later periods. Hubert de Burgh began a ringwork in Kerry Woods in 1228 and in the 1280s the newly founded towns beside the Severn at Llanidloes and Newtown were each given a large but low mound with timber buildings to protect the side away from the river. Another type only occasionally found in Mid Wales is the quadrangular water filled moat around a platform 30 to 60m long. These mark the sites of manor houses and rectories not otherwise fortified except for a small site at Hen Castell where there is debris of a former thick curtain wall. In most cases the internal buildings were constructed of perishable materials. Moats were not necessarily defensive. They were status symbols of the upper class being scenic features able to provide a habitat for fish, eels, and water fowl, which together formed a large part of the diet of the gentry. Moats also kept out wild animals and vagrants and kept in domestic animals and servants.

Something should be said of some features of the castles. Glass was uncommon in medieval secular buildings, windows being closed with shutters so the rooms were dark when the weather was bad. Some rooms were heated by fires in central hearths with a louvre in the roof. Wall fireplaces survive in the keeps at Tretower, Bronllys, and Hay. Window embrasures often had stone seats. Iron stanchions secured wide openings within easy reach of the ground. Furnishings were sparse and simple. Lords circulated from one castle or manor to another to consume agricultural produce in situ and servants and portable furnishings went with them, leaving only caretakers when there was no need for the expense of a permanent garrison. Internal rooms were often plastered and painted with allegorical or biblical scenes or patterns. Whitewash applied to crudely built outer walls of shale often set in poor mortar helped delay their disintegration. By the 14th century private rooms were provided in towers or ranges built against the curtains but originally there was little privacy and some household members would bed down in the places where they worked like the kitchen or stables or wherever there was a fire.

The Mortimer 2nd Earl of March repaired Montgomery and Bronllys in the 1360s. Like many castles they became rather neglected during the peace until Owain Glyndwr united many of the Welsh behind him in the 1400s and joined a rebellion against Henry IV. Many of the Welsh border castles were captured by the rebels in spite of being repaired and garrisoned. After a full decade of crisis they were allowed to decay again. In 1424 the Mortimer estates passed via an heiress to Richard, Earl of Cambridge, who became Duke of York in 1426. He had little use for many of the remote border strongholds although Cefnllys seems to have been maintained at least until the 1450s. The Dukes of Stafford had inherited Brecon and Hay castles, which they kept in repair, and Bronllys, which was left to decay. Powis Castle was divided between heiresses resulting in the Greys inhabiting and maintaining the inner ward whilst the Suttons, whose chief seat was Dudley Castle in Staffordshire, allowed the ranges in the outer ward to decay. The conflicts of 1455 to 1485 left the castles unaffected and at Tretower the Bluets and their successors the Vaughans were content to live in an undefended manor house not far from the crumbling castle. The Vaughans did add a gatehouse and an embattled wall with arrow loops on one side of the house in the 1480s but these were evidently just status symbols for show rather than for defence, and the other sides of the house lacked any such features. They built a similar gatehouse at Great Porthaml and the Herberts built another at their house of Cwrt-Y-Carw at Crickhowell.

Tretower Court

In the 1530s the gatehouse at New Radnor was patched up for use as a county gaol, and Montgomery Castle was repaired to serve as a military and administrative centre. The great hall at Brecon used for county court sessions was re-roofed c1550. New mansions were built in the courtyards at Pencelli in the 1580s, Montgomery in the 1620s, and Hay in the 1660s. Brecon, New Radnor, and Powis castles were captured and slighted by Parliamentary troops during the Civil War. Montgomery was slighted without having to withstand a siege.

Long periods of decay combined with a tendency for rather weak construction has led to little fabric surviving of most castles in Mid Wales. The stone castles of Radnorshire are mostly reduced to buried footings awaiting the archeologist's spade. Montgomeryshire has Powis Castle surviving habitable in a very altered state and the lower parts of Montgomery and Dolforwyn castles now exposed to view by excavations by the Welsh Office. More remains in the county of Brecon where the heavily remodelled tower houses at Scethrog and Talgarth remain habitable, and there are ruins at Brecon, Bronllys, Crickhowell, Blaenllynfi, Hay, Llanddew, Tretower, and Castell Du. A few features such as the gatehouse at Pencelli which have gone since the 18th century are luckily recorded on old engravings and paintings, and in the descriptions by antiquarians and tourists.

Bronllys Castle in 1741

GAZETTEER OF CASTLES IN BRECONSHIRE

ABERLLYNFI CASTLE   SO 171380

A natural platform about 48m long by 30m wide which rises 4m above what was formerly marshland and which must have been divided from the level ground to the east by a ditch forms a bailey. A motte 2m high with a summit 15m across lies at the west end, where there is a stream. The castle was mentioned in documents of the period 1180-1211 and in September 1233 was given by Henry III to Inges, one of his crossbowmen. The castle was recovered soon afterwards by Hugh Kinnersley, its original owner, who fortified it on behalf of his lord Walter de Clifford, who was then in rebellion. Henry III told Henry de Turberville to recapture the castle.

ABERYSCIR MOTTE   SO 000296

A motte lies in trees above the junction of the Usk and Afon Yscir.

ALEXANDERSTONE MOTTES   SO 073301 & 070297

Alexanderstone Farm cuts into the SE side of a motte about 5m high which has traces of a bailey 30m by 15m on the west side. Beside a stream 1.5km to the south is a second very feeble mound.

BLAENCAMLAIS CASTLE   SN 956261

This building is alternatively known as the castle of Cwm Camlais, Maescar, or Defynoch. It may have been the new castle beyond Brecon captured by Prince Edward after his escape from captivity in 1265, and thus the builder would have been Humphrey VI de Bohun. Otherwise it may have been built by Humphrey VII de Bohun immediately after he succeeded as Earl of Hereford in 1275 to serve as a forester's lodge also acting as an outpost of Brecon Castle. A large mound with a ditch and counterscarp, but no bailey, set near the edge of a flat moorland north of Brecon Beacons bears the base of a massive round tower nearly 13m in external diameter. Walling 2m high inside and over 3m thick survives on the west side. The tower is clearly 13th century work but the earthworks may be of 12th century origin.

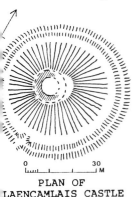

```
0                    30
└┴┴┴┴┴──┴────┴────┘ M
```

PLAN OF
LAENCAMLAIS CASTLE

*Blaencamlais
Castle*

Hall Block, Brecon Castle

BRECON CASTLE

SO 043288

In 1093 Bernard de Newmarch built a castle on the promontory above the confluence of the Usk and Honddu rivers. He was blockaded there by the Welsh in 1094 until relieved by Roger de Newburgh. A rampart and ditch defended a spade-shaped bailey 120m long by 90m wide from the higher ground to the north where the original Norman town lay, and a large mound was raised in the NE corner. Bernard's grandson Roger, Earl of Hereford, died without issue in 1156 and Brecon went to his younger sister Bertha, wife of Philip de Braose. Under him the settlement east of the Honddu was probably laid out and either he or his son William erected a polygonal shell wall on the motte. William fell out with King John in 1207 and lost the castle but it was recaptured by his brothers Giles and Reginald in 1215.

Llywelyn Fawr attacked Brecon in 1217, 1231, and 1233, the new town being destroyed on the latter occasion. Stone walls around the bailey were probably begun immediately afterwards and continued by Humphrey VI de Bohun, heir of the Earl of Hereford, who married the heiress Eleanor de Braose in 1241. The castle was among the several fortresses captured by Prince Edward after his escape from Simon de Montfort's forces in 1265. At about this time Llywelyn ap Gruffudd occupied the district but may not have captured the castle. In 1273 he was besieging Humphrey VII de Bohun there. Edward II took over the castle after Humphrey VIII, the probable builder of the hall block, was killed in 1322 fighting against him at Boroughbridge.

Henry, Duke of Lancaster, married Mary, heiress of Humphrey X de Bohun, who died in 1372. He seized the throne as Henry IV in 1399. Sir Thomas Berkeley held Brecon Castle for him against Owain Glyndwr and in 1404 Lord Berkeley and the Earl of Warwick were sent with 100 men-at-arms and 11 mounted archers to secure the castle. Brecon later passed to the Stafford Dukes of Buckingham, and the name Ely Tower given to the keep refers to Morton, Bishop of Ely, a captive within it during Richard III's reign. The castle hall was given a magnificent new roof in c1550 but it was dismantled in James I's reign. Charles I was at Brecon in August 1645 but soon afterwards Colonel Turberville surrendered the castle after a short siege by Major General Laugharne. The defences were probably then slighted.

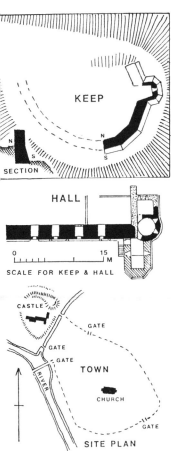

KEEP

SECTION

HALL

0   15
SCALE FOR KEEP & HALL
M

CASTLE

GATE

GATE

GATE

RIVER

TOWN

CHURCH

GATE

SITE PLAN

PLANS OF BRECON CASTLE

Brecon Castle from the East

The mound now lies within the grounds of a house and its slopes have been terraced and planted. On the summit there survive three short sides of a multi-sided shell wall 1.7m thick above a battered plinth around an ovoid court 15m wide. Footings of a fourth side lie beyond a polygonal NE turret of later date containing a vaulted chamber with one tiny loop. Adjoining the hotel south of the mound is the south wall of a hall block of c1300 with two levels of fine apartments above low cellars. Only the cusped single light upper windows are unrestored. The wall is 21m long and 2.4m thick above a plinth and ends on the east in a round turret against which abuts a slightly later semi-polygonal latrine turret. The Buck brothers' engraving shows defensive walls further south, perhaps of a lower bailey, but these do not appear on Meredith Jones' plan of 1744. He shows the castle as having a gatehouse facing NW and a round tower keep within the shell wall as at Tretower, which is quite likely.

Jones also shows the layout of the now-destroyed 13th century town walls which were flanked by ten D-shaped towers and had four gates, destroyed in 1785. Two of them lay close together facing the bridges over the Usk and Honddu, the Struet Gate lay on the north side, and the Watton Gate lay at the SE end of the town. The line of the walls, which were repaired in 1404, is still fairly clear.

BRONLLYS CASTLE

Richard Fitz Pons established a castle here in the 1090s, creating a motte against a rock outcrop above the Afon Llynfi with an inner bailey of triangular shape extending 60m northwards with a wider outer bailey beyond. Giraldus Cambrensis mentions a stone falling from a tower at Bronllys in a fire in 1175, but the existing round tower keep on the motte and the now vanished inner bailey curtain were built by Walter de Clifford II after the castle had been burnt by the Welsh in 1233. The castle was later held by the Mortimers and was taken from them by Edward II in 1322. It was later restored to the 2nd Earl of March who remodelled the upper part of the keep in the 1360s. Anne Stafford successfully claimed the castle during Henry VI's reign but it was later returned to the Crown and left to decay. It was given to Humphrey Stafford, 3rd Duke of Buckingham, in 1508, and was said to be abandoned and ruined in 1521 when his estates were surveyed after his execution. Henry VIII then gave Bronllys to Sir David Williams but before long Sir Roger Vaughan of Porthaml had obtained the estate which was later held in turn by the families of Knollys, Cecil, Morgan, Williams, Lewis, and Davies. Part of the hall in the bailey, shown on the Bucks' engraving, was incorporated into the stable block of a new house built in the 1790s.

The ruined keep is in State guardianship. It measures 9.8m in diameter above a high battered plinth capped by a roll-moulding and is over 16m high. The entrance doorway has a drawbar hole and leads into a hall 5.2m in diameter with two window embrasures. One has a stair leading down towards the vaulted cellar below, although the last 3m of the drop to the floor has to be reached by a ladder. A stair curves round from the side of the other embrasure up to the private chamber above with two embrasures with ogee-headed windows and a fireplace. Another stair leads to the more ruined top storey with a fireplace and three evenly spaced embrasures with seats.

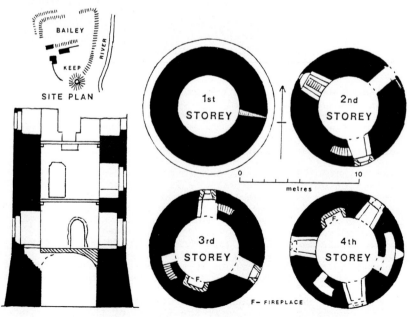

PLANS & SECTION OF THE KEEP, BRONLLYS CASTLE

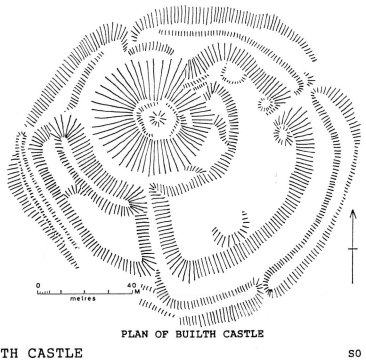

PLAN OF BUILTH CASTLE

BUILTH CASTLE   SO 044510

The impressive earthworks rising high above the Wye east of Builth
Wells are relics of a castle built in c1095 by Philip de Braose. A
motte rises 9m above a ditch 2m deep to a summit 17m across. A 90m
long and 30m wide crescent-shaped bailey lies to the east and south
and a smaller outer bailey lies to the west. A deep ditch with a
high counterscarp bank surrounds the whole of the circular area.
     Rhys ap Gruffudd captured the castle in 1168. Giles and Reginald
de Braose recaptured the castle from King John in 1215 and began to
refortify it. After John died they made their peace with the Crown
and Henry III aided the construction of further defensive works at
Builth by Reginald in 1219. Llywelyn Fawr failed to capture the
castle by siege in 1223, but it was surrendered to him in 1229 after
he had captured William de Braose. After Llywelyn executed William
in 1230 Builth passed via an heiress Maud to the Mortimers. Henry
III began rebuilding the castle in stone in 1242. In 1260 Llywelyn
ap Gruffudd failed in an attempt to storm the castle, but it was
betrayed to him shortly afterwards and then destroyed.
     Edward I had the castle rebuilt between 1277 and 1283 probably
to a design by James of St George. In all some £1,834 was spent on
the works. There appears to have been a large round tower keep on
the motte, possibly built on the base of a similar structure built
in the 1240s, and it was probably surrounded by a low chemise wall.
The inner bailey had a curtain wall flanked by six D-shaped towers
and a twin-towered gatehouse. A force of 9 horsemen and 40 foot
formed the garrison in 1277, although it was reduced the next year.
In 1283 Llywelyn ap Gruffudd was killed in a skirmish nearby after
unsuccessfully trying to persuade the garrison to yield the castle
to him. The Prince's death removed the immediate threat to central
Wales and the works at Builth came to a halt. Probably the curtain
of the west bailey was never built, and the gatehouse of the inner
bailey was perhaps not finished as intended.

Builth Castle

During the Welsh revolt of 1294 Builth Castle was held by John Giffard and manned by three heavily armed horsemen, three lightly armed horsemen, 20 crossbowmen, and 40 longbowmen. The de Bohuns held the castle in 1317 and they claimed custody of it in Edward III's reign, although it was actually held by various families for short periods, having been confiscated by Edward II in 1322 after the Earl of Hereford was killed at Boroughbridge. The castle was probably abandoned in the latter part of the 15th century and most of the stonework later removed for construction of buildings in the town. Excavation of the castle site is most desirable.

CAER BERIS MOTTE
SO 030507

Guarding the neck of a loop of the River Irfon just 1km west of Builth Wells is a mound rising 6m to a summit 22m long by 18m wide. A house of 1896-1911 lies within the site of the bailey.

CAERAU MOTTE
SN 923501

There are slight traces of a mound by a farm on a Roman fort site.

CASTELL BLAENLLYNFI
SO 145229

Hidden in woodland are fragments of the walls and the now dried up moat of a castle of the Mortimer family probably built in the late 12th century. The castle was captured in 1215 by Giles and Reginald de Braose and in 1233 by Richard Marshal, Earl of Pembroke. It was among the Mortimer possessions confiscated by Edward II in 1322. The castle formed a rectangle 67m from east to west by about 50m from north to south within a curtain wall 1.8m thick of shale laid in a poor mortar. The footings of the south side remain and a high section on the east. At the SE corner are footings of a rectangular tower about 10m by 8m externally set diagonally and mid-way along the east side are traces of a round tower about 7.2m in diameter. This tower, and the footings of a similar one found by excavation at the SW corner, were additions either of c1235-45 or the 1260s. Two buttresses west of the latter, and another east of it, have survived better than the sections of wall to which they were added. There are indications of domestic buildings on the west and north sides, and the lower part of what was probably a hall block 16m by 7m in the middle of the south side. The moat was held in by a dam to the NW and north. There are traces of an outer court to the SE.

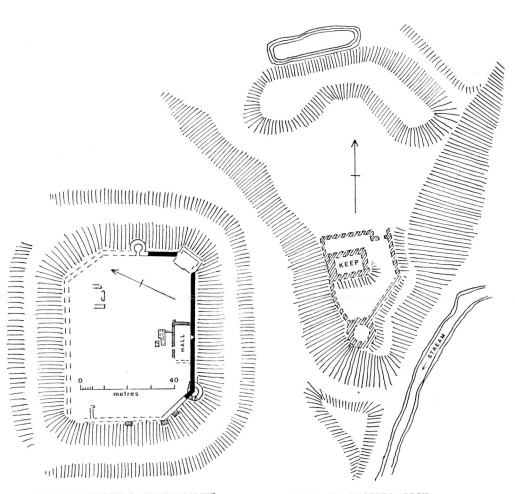

PLAN OF CASTELL BLAENLLYNFI   PLAN OF CASTELL COCH

CASTELL COCH   SN 936144

This castle taking its name from the red sandstone of which it is
built lies on a promontory about 9m high between the Afon Llia and
Afon Dringarth in a remote position on the south side of the Brecon
Beacons. The only historical reference to it is in 1239 when it was
held by William de Braose. The southern end of the promontory has
beneath a tangle of vegetation the last vestiges of a wall about
1.5m thick around a pentangular court about 27m wide. Adjoining the
west wall and occupying much of the rectangular northern part of
the court is a keep about 16m long by 12m wide. At the NE corner are
signs of a recessed gateway. The southern part of the court tapers
to an acute angle which was occupied by a round tower about 13m in
external diameter, large enough to form a second keep. The layout
and poor quality of the masonry suggest it may date from the 1260s
when Llywelyn ap Gruffudd controlled this area. North of the court
is a bailey 60m wide protected on the north side by a high rampart
with a ditch in front of it, half of which is water filled.

CASTELL DINAS

Castell Dinas formed the chief seat of the lordship of Blaenllynfi.
It lies at 450m upon a foothill of the Black Mountains and is the
highest castle site in Britain. Dinas may be the 'Waynard's Castle'
mentioned in 1143-55. Early in Henry III's reign when Reginald de
Braose was reconciled with Llywelyn Fawr the English King took over
the castles of Blaenllynfi, Talgarth, and Dinas and granted them to
Peter FitzHerbert. De Braose took them back but FitzHerbert obtained
a better title to the castles by marrying one of the heiresses of
William de Braose after the latter's execution by Llywelyn. In 1234
Dinas was among the castles captured by Richard Marshal, Earl of
Pembroke, and Llywelyn. All of FitzHerbert's sons died in the 1240s
and Henry III granted Blaenllynfi and Dinas to Walerand de Teys.
Subsequently, under the Mortimers, Blaenllynfi was developed as a
residence and Dinas left to decay although Owain Glyndwr may have
used it as a base in the 1400s. It may been deliberately destroyed
in the 15th century as Leland in c1540 describes it as it is now.
Although little remains apart from buried footings and debris
the site is of interest as being a castle of some size with walls,
towers, and a keep all likely to predate the building boom of the
1230s and 40s when many castles of the Welsh Marches were rebuilt
in stone. A ditch cuts an eye-shaped Iron Age hillfort 180m long by
83m wide into two baileys. The northern bailey was surrounded by a
wall up to 2m thick which still remains in a very ruinous state as
part of a modern boundary on the lower east side. At the north end
was a re-entrant angle with a postern gateway flanked by a small
tower on the south side and protected externally by a barbican. The
tower is the only part of the ruins where walling not obscured by
debris stands above footings, and a damaged pointed arched opening
survives facing the court. The highest part of the bailey is the
SW corner which is filled by an inner ward which is very roughly a
square of 38m and has signs of a gatehouse on the south, a SW tower
and a NW tower, east of which was a second gateway. The west wall
remains indicate a thickness of about 2.5m. The internal height to
the wall-walk may only have been about 3m but the external height
would have been much greater. The eastern half of the inner ward is
occupied by the remains of a rectangular keep about 20m long by 15m
wide within a chemise wall enclosing a court 26m by 20m, between
which and the south gate were a range of domestic buildings. The
whole of the hilltop is surrounded by a deep ditch and counterscarp.

Postern Gateway, Castell Dinas

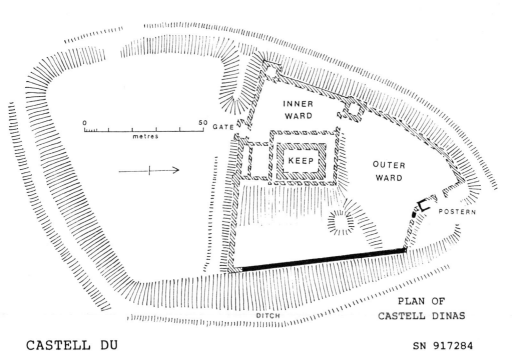

PLAN OF
CASTELL DINAS

0 ——— 50
metres

INNER
WARD

GATE

KEEP

OUTER
WARD

POSTERN

DITCH

CASTELL DU   SN 917284

Only fragments of the south wall of a courtyard with a projecting
round tower about 7.8m in diameter now survive of a 13th century
castle alternatively known as Castell Rhyd-Y-Briw. This may have
been the castle begun by Llywelyn ap Gruffudd in 1262, and in 1271
was occupied by his ally Einion Sais, who is traditionally said to
have had a second castle at Penpont where a tributary stream flows
into the River Usk halfway between Castell Du and Brecon.

CASTLE MADOC   SO 125370

The Powell family constructed a ringwork about 25m in diameter in
c1095-1120. The rampart may have been slighted towards the approach
on the south when they later built a motte and bailey castle on the
lower ground to the SW. The motte rises 6m above a ditch with a 3m
high counterscarp on the east. The summit measures 22m east-west by
18m north-south. The bailey south of the motte is said to have been
given a curtain wall in the 14th century but there are no obvious
remains of such. The bailey site is now occupied by a house bearing
a datestone of 1588 with the initials of Thomas Powell. This was
remodelled in the late 17th century and has 19th century additions.

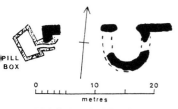

PILL
BOX

0 ——— 10 ——— 20
metres

PLAN OF CASTELL DU

Castell Du

17

CILWHYBERT MOTTE
SO 014268

Immediately north of a farm is a fine motte rising 7m from a ditch 2m deep which was water filled except on the south earlier in this century when the mound was overgrown. The summit is 13m in diameter.

CLAWYD BRITISH MOTTE
SO 862369

A ringwork measuring 42m by 30m with a rampart 2.5m high above the ditch lies in an isolated and elevated position by Halfway Forest.

CRICKADARN RINGWORKS
SO 088421 & 059413

Not far west of the church is a D-shaped ringwork with a ditch 3 or 4m deep all round except towards the main ridge where it may have been filled in. The straight NW side overlooks a slope. The other sides had some protection from marshland. Another D-shaped ringwork lies above a slope 2km to the west at 360m. It has a rampart and ditch which are pierced for an entrance on the SE side.

CRICKHOWELL CASTLE
SO 218183

Early in the 12th century the Turbervilles probably supplemented Maes Celyn motte with a large new motte and bailey castle on this low lying site slightly above the Usk. Rebuilding in masonry began under Sir Grimbald Pauncefoot of Gloucestershire who married Sybil Turberville in c1264, and continued after his death in 1287 by his sons Grimbald, who died in 1315, and Emeric, who was dispossessed by Edward II in 1322 for his support of the Mortimers. The castle has an alternative name of Alisby's Castle after another of the knights serving Roger Mortimer. Emeric's son Sir Grimbald recovered the castle and his brother Hugh's son John held it against Glyndwr in 1403. When the Pauncefoot line ended in the mid 15th century the castle was claimed by Richard, Duke of York, who married a Mortimer heiress. His son Edward IV granted Crickhowell to his supporter Sir William Herbert. By that time the castle may have been in decay and the buildings were subsequently robbed for buildings in the town.

The mound bears the last traces of an shell keep enclosing a court about 24m long by 15m wide. It was reached by steps from the NW corner of a bailey about 55m square. The foot of the steps was guarded by a barbican with round towers 6m in diameter flanking a drawbridge pit. The bases of the towers remain and the NW quadrant of the western tower survives to full height showing evidence of a basement, two upper storeys with fireplaces, and battlements. Old drawings show that the now vanished bailey walls had a square tower at the SE corner and a round tower at the SW corner. The NE corner still has a round tower 8m in diameter still standing three storeys high with battlements. It may have formed part of the gatehouse. Adjoining it to the south is a rectangular tower of slightly later date which was at least 10m long by 5.6m wide externally. Only the north wall now survives above the level of the lowest of the four storeys. The bailey walls must have been substantially complete by 1281 when the town obtained a murage grant for building walls which have not survived. The folly tower of much later date standing in Tower Street has no connection with the castle or town defences. A drawing of 1805 by Hoare shows the castle much as it is now except that he appears to show a broad wet moat east of the castle bailey.

GARN COCH MOTTE
SO 213477

The small motte on a flat, low lying site, is almost worn away.

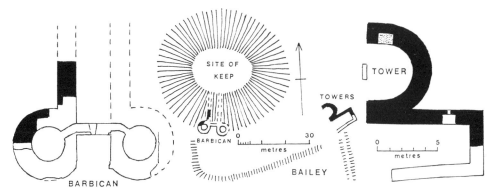

PLANS OF CRICKHOWELL CASTLE

GARN-Y-CASTELL

SO 158297

The very worn down ringwork 1.5m high and 30m across on a spur 2km west of Castell Dinas is a possible alternative site for Waynard's Castle, mentioned in a charter of 1143-55 of the Earl of Hereford.

Barbican Tower, Crickhowell

Crickhowell Castle

HAY CASTLE

The motte rising 3m to a summit 20m across near the parish church SW of the town is probably the site of the 'castello de haia' which is mentioned in 1121. It was probably built by William Revel, one of Bernard de Newmarch's knights. Later in the 12th century a more commanding site to the NE was utilised for a large oval ringwork 85m by 70m. Matilda de Braose is said to have built the stone keep in c1200 but it is perhaps more likely that she added the gateway arch to a tower built in the 1180s. She died of starvation at the command of King John, who burnt the castle and town of Hay in 1216 while attempting to suppress the rebellion of Giles and Reginald de Braose. They were burnt again by Llywelyn Fawr in 1231 and had to rebuilt by Henry III. In 1232 and 1237 he granted the townsfolk of Hay the right to collect a special toll to pay for walling in the town with stone. The castle was captured by Prince Edward in 1264 and by Simon de Montfort's forces in 1265.

Both town and castle suffered damage by Owain Glyndwr's forces in 1400 but the castle was listed as defensible against the Welsh in 1403. The castle had passed to the Earls of Stafford, later Dukes of Buckingham, and is said to have suffered further damage during the conflicts of the 1460s. The last Duke, executed by Henry VIII in 1521, remodelled the keep. Whatever apartments then adjoined it were swept away in the 1660s when James Boyle of Hereford built a new mansion. Most of the curtain wall was either demolished during the Civil War or later to improve the views from the mansion. In the early 19th century the house was occupied by the Wellington family who purchased it from Glyn heiresses. The house was restored c1910 but the eastern part was gutted by fire in 1939. The western part was gutted by a second fire in 1979 but has been restored. It and various outbuildings are now used for second-hand book selling.

The keep measures 10m from north to south by 8.3m wide. There is a small cellar only a third of the size of the three storeys of rooms above it. Access to it must have been by a hatch and ladder. The lowest habitable room has the remains of a Late Norman window of two lights facing the court and above it is a better preserved specimen, lacking only the mullion between the two round arched lights set in an outer round arch. No other original features now survive and there is no stair, there being little room for such a feature within the thin walls. At some time the northern corners were provided with heavy buttressing and in c1500 the north wall was given wooden lintelled fireplaces serving the lower two habitable rooms with on either side two light windows with wooden lintelled embrasures. In an earlier rebuilding, probably after some damage caused by the Welsh in 1231, the whole SE corner was replaced and buttressed, and a new doorway made alongside it facing east. At the same time the outer arch of the gateway was added, providing the slot for a portcullis worked from a small chamber at the height of the wall-walk about 7m above the court. The wall-walk, portcullis room, and keep doorway are reached by a stair beside the keep SE corner which turns to rise over the back of the gateway. The 12m long section of curtain east of the gateway is all that remains of the wall around the courtyard which was about 75m from east to west by 65m wide. The wall is 1.8m thick at the top but is more like 3.0m thick at the base where it has a high plinth of complex form.

The town walls enclosed a D-shaped area with the straight side facing the Wye. The castle lay on the south side with the West Gate nearby. To the east was the Black Lion Gate and to the north the Water Gate, all removed in the late 18th century. The last sections of the wall on the west were removed for the railway in the 1860s.

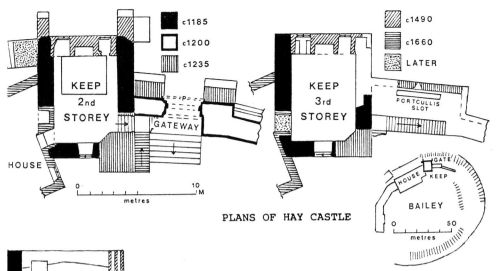

PLANS OF HAY CASTLE

c1185
c1200
c1235
c1490
c1660
LATER

KEEP 2nd STOREY

HOUSE

GATEWAY

0 10 M

metres

KEEP 3rd STOREY

PORTCULLIS SLOT

GATE
HOUSE KEEP
BAILEY

0 50

metres

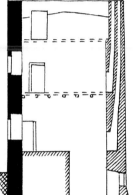

KEEP SECTION

Hay Castle from the South

Hay Motte

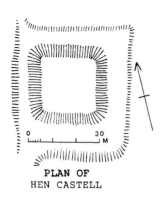

PLAN OF
HEN CASTELL

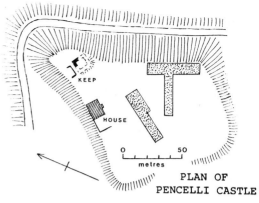

PLAN OF
PENCELLI CASTLE

HEN CASTELL

SO 213166

An overgrown moated and stone-revetted platform about 22m square
and 2m high upon the hillside SE of Llangattock is all that remains
of a 14th century manor house enclosed by a thick curtain wall.

LLANAFAN MOTTE

SN 967566

SW of the church is a ringwork with an outer ditch and bank.

LLANDDEW PALACE

SO 055308

In the grounds of the vicarage north of Llanddew church are remains
of a palace built by Bishop Gower of St Davids in c1340 on the site
of a residence of Giraldus Cambrensis in the 1170s. It was probably
here in 1291 that the Earls of Gloucester and Hereford were tried
for conducting their private war over possession of the northern
part of Senghennydd. There are ivy-mantled ruins of a hall block 20m
long by 10.5m wide over walls 1.2m thick on the NW and a ditch on
the NE. On the west is part of a curtain wall with a well set under
a cambered arch, and on the SW is a rough revetment 2.5m high. Part
of a small round solid turret also remained a few years ago.

Llanddew Palace

22

LLANDEFAELOG FACH MOTTE   SO 033323

West of the church is a tree-clad motte rising 3m above the ground
to the south where a house of 1630 stands on the site of the bailey
and much more above the stream to the north. The top is 15m across.

LLANLEONFEL MOTTE   SN 919520

The small rectangular court is enclosed by a rampart and rock-cut
ditch on the three sides away from the steep drop on the north.

LLANTHOMAS MOTTE   SO 209403

A worn down motte damaged on the west side lies beside the Digedi
Brook. There are signs of a surrounding ditch.

LLYSDINAM MOTTE   SN 998584

A ringwork lies on a spur high above the Estyn Brook.

MAES CELYN MOTTE   SO 095248

This tree-clad mound with the last traces of a stone tower about 9m
square on the higher of two levels on the summit was an outwork
or predecessor of Crickhowell Castle 1.5km to the SE.

PENCELLI CASTLE   SO 095248

Pencelli Castle was built by one of Bernard de Newmarch's knights
in the 1090s. It was the seat of an important lordship originally
owing four and a half knights fees towards the defence of the castle
of Brecon. The castle was captured by Giles and Reginald de Braose
in 1215 and by Richard Marshal in 1233. Reginald later settled the
castle upon his wife Gwladys Ddu, the daughter of Llywelyn Fawr,
in return for Kerry and Cedewain. She later married Ralph Mortimer
who claimed Pencelli. The dispute was only finally settled when one
of William de Braose's daughters married Ralph's son Roger, who
probably built a new curtain wall and gatehouse at Pencelli in the
1270s. The castle was confiscated by Edward II in 1322 and given to
Hugh Despenser the younger. It was later a Crown possession until
Edward IV granted it to the Herberts. A new house was built in the
late 16th century to replace the delapidated domestic buildings.
Richard Herbert sold Pencelli to his brother-in-law Captain Thomas
Powell of Llanishen in the late 17th century.
   The castle originally seems to have consisted of a ringwork at
the projecting north corner, strongly defended by natural slopes,
of a rectangular bailey 110m long by 90m wide. The ringwork was by
the end of the 12th century superseded by a massive tower keep 15m
square of which parts of the NE and NW walls can still be seen in
a clump of trees and shrubs together with part of a second building.
The Buck brothers' view of 1741 shows two walls of the keep still
standing three storeys high. In front of it they show a gatehouse
with twin round towers and a fragment of a curtain wall with a pair
of lancet windows. Nothing now remains of these but the house also
shown is still inhabited. It bears the year 1583 on the main door
and may be largely of that date. It is, however, much altered, and
has re-set medieval material, including a 15th century window with
a segmental head, and parts of two Late Norman windows with grooved
heads, one of which has been set upside down.

PYTINDU MOTTE   SO 047310

Castle mounds once lay at the farms of Pytindu and Pytingwyn.

Scethrog Tower

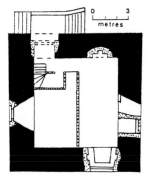
PLAN OF SCETHROG TOWER

SCETHROG TOWER

SO 105249

On flat ground beside the Usk is a much altered tower built by the descendants of Milo Picard in the early 14th century. There are a few traces of a moated enclosure to the west but no other medieval walls or outbuildings survive. The tower measures about 11m square over walls 2m thick which are battered for much of their height. Above a low cellar which has long been inaccessible are a room set a few steps up from ground level and an upper storey, plus attics in the gabled roof. Originally there was probably a third storey although it may have been in the form of an attic within a parapet. The only original features are an altered upper storey fireplace and a pointed doorway to a now disused staircase which probably led up to the lost battlements. The other features are of the 16th and 17th centuries and the dividing walls of the rooms are still later.

Talgarth Tower

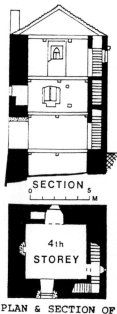
SECTION

4th STOREY

PLAN & SECTION OF
TALGARTH TOWER

TALGARTH TOWER

SO 154337

On the east bank of the stream running through Talgarth village is a much altered tower probably built in the 14th century. There are no signs of any original adjoining buildings or a courtyard nor is anything known about who may have built the structure. It measures 8.2m by 7.8m and rises 9.5m to the eaves of a late 17th or early 18th century pyramidal roof which has probably replaced a parapet. The tower has a low cellar below the ground level to the east and three upper storeys connected by straight staircases in the NE end wall. Modern buildings adjoin both end walls and have obscured the original entrance arrangements but the doorway is likely to have been in the NE wall one stage above ground level. The fireplaces are later replacements but original latrines and pointed windows with embrasures with seats remain in the side walls.

TRECASTLE MOTTE

SN 882292

This is the best preserved motte and bailey castle in the county of Breconshire. An oval tree-clad motte 6m high occupies the east half of a bailey platform 115m long by 45m wide.

TREDUSTAN MOTTE

SO 140324

A motte rising 4.5m to a summit 15m across lies behind a farmhouse.

TREFECA MOTTE

SO 145314 & 142323

A house now lies within the bailey which has strong natural slopes on each side except to the SE. The construction of the railway from Hay to Brecon caused removal of most of the motte in the NW corner leaving a chord of the summit 6m long and 2.5m high, now overgrown. A predecessor ringwork 25m across lies on the hillside 1km SE.

Trecastle Motte

Tretower Castle

TRETOWER CASTLE   SO 185213

Picard, one of Bernard de Newmarch's knights, built a modest stone
revetted motte with a triangular bailey surrounded by marshes and
moats fed by the Rhiangoll Brook in c1100. His son Roger in c1160
built a stone shell wall with a hall, solar, and kitchen inside it.
His great grandson Roger Picard in c1230-40 enclosed the bailey with
curtains with two round corner towers with high battered plinths,
and replaced the domestic buildings within the shell wall upon the
motte with a round tower keep. The castle was probably over-run by
the local Welsh in 1263 and the top storey of the keep was perhaps
added afterwards as a more effective observation point.

Tretower Court just 80m to the SE has an east range which may
have been built by John Picard on whose death in 1305 the castle
was said to be worth nothing. So it seems to have been abandoned as
a residence after the Welsh defeat of 1282 although in 1403 it was
refortified against Owain Glyndwr and an early 16th century sketch
suggests the defences were then still intact. Tretower was held by
the Bluet family during the 14th century and then passed by marriage
to James de Berkeley. In 1432 his son Lord Berkeley sold Tretower
to his mother's second husband Sir William ap Thomas. The lordship
and manor still belong to the Duke of Beaufort, a descendant of Sir
William's son William Herbert. The latter, however gave Tretower
Court to his mother Gwladys' eldest son by her first marriage, Sir
Roger Vaughan, who became a leading dignitary in Breconshire, and
remodelled the house to serve as his residence. In c1480-5 his son
Thomas added the gatehouse and curtain wall on the south side as a
form of status symbol rather than for defence as the house lacked
a moat and had no other defensive features on the other sides.

Further alterations to the house were made by Charles Vaughan
in c1630. The direct male line died out with his grandson Edward
and the Morgans who succeeded and took the name Vaughan eventually
moved elsewhere, leaving the house to be leased as a farm. It was
handed over to the State after purchase by the Brecknock Society.

The shell wall is 1.8m thick above a battered plinth acting as
a retaining wall to the small motte. It is broken down on the north
and on the east where there is the base of a gatehouse 5m deep by
6m wide with a shallow pit below the passageway. The SW corner of
the shell collapsed in 1947. It contained a spiral stair connecting
an office with a solar above of which all that remains are a window
and blocked fireplace in the shell wall. A second window served the
hall to the east. South of the hall was a kitchen in a projection.

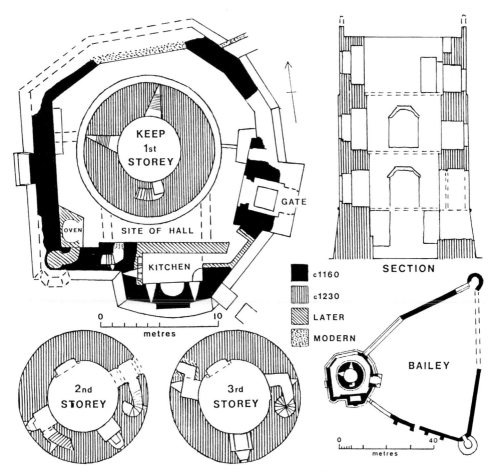

PLANS OF TRETOWER CASTLE

The tower keep in the middle of the shell is 11m in diameter over walls 2.8m thick above a high battered plinth. The entrance passage gives onto a hall with a hooded fireplace and two window embrasures from one of which a stair curves down to a basement lit only with two loops with the sills steeply stepped down. From the entrance passage is a spiral stair to the solar and upper levels. The solar also has a hooded fireplace and two windows. The doorway opening out of one of the embrasures led to a now-destroyed block built against the keep, perhaps during the Glyndwr crisis. The top storey is marked by an external offset which is continued across a staircase loop in the form of a transom. There is no fireplace.

The bailey is now mostly filled with farm buildings. It has a fragmentary wall 1.5m thick. There are foundations of a tower 7.0m diameter at ground level at the south corner and buttresses set against the wall linking it to the shell. More stands of an east tower. The gatehouse probably lay midway between the two towers.

TYMAUR MOTTE   SO 125257

This motte composed of sandstone blocks covered with earth rises 3.5m to a summit with diameters of 15m and 12m.

GAZETTEER OF CASTLES IN MONTGOMERYSHIRE

BISHOP'S MOAT
SO 291896

Elevated at 340m on the border with Shropshire is a motte rising 6m to a summit 13m across on the west side of an oval bailey 100m long by 65m wide. The castle was built by the Bishop of Hereford in c1120 and may be the Castell Hithoet captured in 1233 by Llywelyn Fawr.

BRONFELIN MOTTE
SO 052913

This 4m high mound with a summit 10m across and a triangular bailey 27m wide by 48m long to the NE lie above a steep slope to the NW. They served as an outpost to the larger but more low lying major earthwork castle of Rhos Ddiarbed just 1km to the SW.

BRYN DERWEN MOTTE
SO 163952

The farm lies on the site of a bailey of a big quarried-away motte.

CAER SIAC MOTTE
SO 129972

The oval motte was much damaged when new tracks were made over and beside it in the 1960s, and two baileys have also been destroyed.

CARREGHOFA CASTLE
SJ 255222 or 254218

The earthwork lying above a steep drop to the River Cynllaith may be the site of the castle built in 1101 by Robert de Bellesme and taken by Henry I's forces in 1102. It was repaired and garrisoned by Henry II in 1159-62 and was captured in 1163 by Owain Cyfeiliog and Owain Fychan. It was recovered by Henry II in 1165 but in 1187 the castle was occupied by Owain Fychan. He was slain during a night attack on it by his cousins Gwenwynwyn and Cadwallon. In 1194 the castle was recaptured for the English Crown and then given a stone curtain. It was then of some importance because of nearby silver mining. In 1197 the castle was handed over to Gwenwynwyn in order to secure the release of his prisoner Gruffudd ap Rhys, the ruler of Deheubarth. In 1212-13 Robert de Vipont rebuilt the castle for King John. It is assumed to have been destroyed by Llywelyn Fawr in the 1230s and to have not been restored. A rampart encloses the 27m long north side and 13m long east side of what is now a modest triangular court but which before either collapse or quarrying was probably a rectangle three times as big. An alternative possible site for the stone castle is at Carreghofa Hall to the south where in 1871 a square room with plastered walls and other foundations of unknown date were found below the house and an adjacent field.

CASTLE CAEREINION
SJ 163054

The churchyard seems to have formed the bailey of a much worn down motte in the north corner erected in 1156 by Madoc ap Maredudd. It passed to his nephew Owain Cyfeiliog who went into exile after he took the side of the Normans soon after joining a Welsh alliance. With Norman support he later captured and destroyed the castle and killed all the garrison installed by his cousin Owain Fychan.

CASTELL MOCH
SJ 112246

The damaged motte by a farm probably had a summit diameter of 23m.

CEFNBRYNTALCH MOTTE
SO 175963

A rocky hilltop 21m wide is divided into inner and outer enclosures 33m and 40m long respectively with an approach on the SW side.

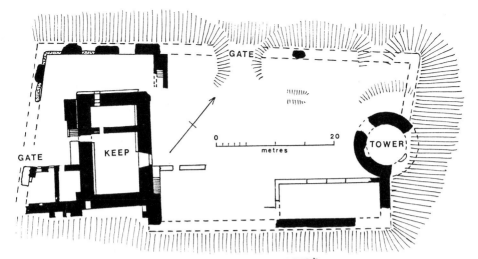

PLAN OF DOLFORWYN CASTLE

DOLFORWYN CASTLE   SO 153950

Llywelyn ap Gruffudd had this castle under construction in 1273 as
a snub to the authority of the English Crown, which had a castle at
Montgomery 7km to the east, and to help keep the Prince of Powys in
check. The work was probably well advanced by 1274 when Llywelyn
stayed at the castle and while there discovered that the Prince of
Powys (no doubt upset by the building of Dolforwyn) was party to a
plot against him. The Prince of Powys was given custody of Dolforwyn
after it was surrendered to Henry Lacy and Roger Mortimer in April
1277 following Llywelyn's failure to relieve a siege against the
castle. An inventory of 1322, when Edward II's forces seized it from
Roger Mortimer, mentions a chapel, hall, lady's chamber, bakehouse,
kitchen, and brewery. The castle is unlikely to have been much used
afterwards and is said to have been ruinous by the 1390s.

Dolforwyn Castle

29

Dolforwyn Castle

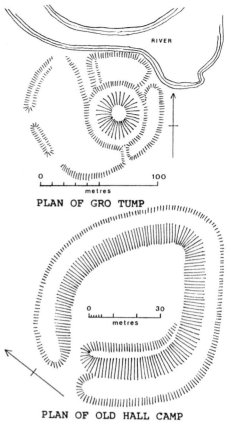

PLAN OF GRO TUMP

PLAN OF OLD HALL CAMP

The castle remains and the slight traces of a town founded at the same time lie on a wooden ridge above the Severn near Abermule. recent excavations by the Welsh Office, who now have custody of the site, have revealed the lower parts of most of the walls of which only a few higher fragments were formerly visible. The design of the castle is decidedly archaic for an important fortress of c1270. A wall 1.7m thick pierced probably by gates on the SW and NW sides surrounds a court 65m long by 28m wide. The longest and naturally best defended sides were totally lacking in any towers or turrets to provide flanking fire but set astride the line of the NE wall is a tower 11m in diameter over walls 2.2m thick. The SW third of the court is mostly filled by a rectangular keep with a domestic range SW of it and there was probably another range taking up most of the space NW of the keep. The keep measures 19m long by 12.3m over 2.2m thick walls. The basement has a doorway on the SW next to the foot of an external stair to the destroyed upper storey. The very large window on the SE side must surely be a later insertion to make the room more use for living in rather than just for storage and it was perhaps then that the NW end was divided off to make a strongroom. In the south corner is a shoot for a latrine at the level of the main hall above. Two other shoots serving latrines in the uppermost rooms of the adjoining range lie nearby and beside the east corner is a shoot from a latrine on the curtain wall-walk which was reached by an external stair beside this corner. There are indications that the whole of the rest of the SE side of the court between the keep and the round tower was filled with spacious rooms or offices.

*Hen
Domen*

GRO TUMP
SO 123922

Beside a golf course east of Newtown is a very impressive motte and bailey castle probably built in the 1080s by Roger de Montgomery. The inner bailey 18m wide by 38m long is strongly protected by the steep falls to the River Severn on the north and east, the 9m high motte with a summit diameter of 11m to the south, and a rampart on the west rising 5m above a ditch 2m deep. An outer bailey 30m wide on the south and 45m wide on the west where there is a rampart 2m high protects the outer sides of the motte away from the river.

HEN DOMEN
SJ 241188

This mound in a commanding position has been damaged by badgers. It rises 6m to an irregular shaped and eroded summit 13m in diameter.

HEN DOMEN
SO 214981

This was the original Montgomery Castle recorded in the Shropshire part of Domesday Book of 1086 as being held by Roger de Montgomery who probably erected it in c1075. Extensive excavations have shown that the timber buildings were rebuilt many times until finally abandoned in c1300. Traces of no less than five successive bridges up to the 16m diameter motte summit were found. The bailey is 50m wide and extends 38m east of the motte ditch. A high counterscarp bank surrounds the whole castle except on the south where a modern road has caused its removal. On the west it has its own outer ditch. In c1105 Henry I granted the castle to Baldwin de Bollers and his descendants held it until 1207. It was taken by the Welsh in 1214.

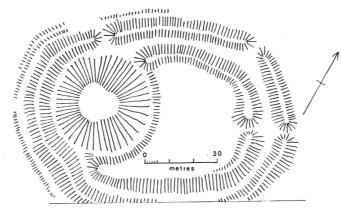

PLAN OF HEN DOMEN

HYSSINGTON CASTLE

SO 315945

The small hill SE of the church with a steep slope on the NE side has been formed into a triangular bailey 70m long by 45m wide. The buried base of a tower 9m square on a low mound occupies the north corner and traces have been seen in the east corner of a probable hall block 18m by 9m externally plus another building. Ruins still stood in 1811. This site is perhaps more likely than Symon's Castle 3km to the WSW to be the castle of Snead occupied by Simon de Parcio in 1231 and given by Henry III to William de Bowles in 1233.

KERRY MOTTE

SO 147895

The overgrown mound on a hillock south of the village was built by Madog ap Idnerth in c1135 to counter the power of the Mortimers. It rises 7m above the ditch on the NW side where a comma-shaped bailey 38m by 24m lies beyond and has a summit diameter of about 10m.

LLANDRINIO MOTTE

SJ 294168

On the bank of the Severn 400m SSW of the church lay a small motte and bailey. The remains are now hidden within a modern flood bank.

LLANFECHAIN MOTTE

SJ 186202

The mound above the Afon Cain SW of the village is likely to have been built by Owain Fychan ap Madog who captured Mochnant in 1166. The mound rises 6m above a ditch with a counterscarp bank to a flat summit 12m across. A shovel-shaped bailey 45m long by 35m wide on the NE has a natural slope to the north and east, a ditch to the west, and on the south a rampart rising 2m above a ditch 1m deep.

LLANGADFAN MOTTE

SJ 012107

Overlooking the Banwy west of the Cann Office Hotel is a remnant of a motte. The hotel lies on the site of the bailey 34m by 30m with an entrance on the south facing a loop of the river.

LLANIDLOES CASTLE

SN 954844

After Owain de la Pole was granted a charter in 1280 for a market at Llanidloes the town was laid out on a rectangular plan beside the Severn with a rampart and ditch on the north and east sides, and gates in the middle of each of the west, north, and east sides. The south side was closed off by a castle of earth and wood. It had a moated mound 30m across on top and 3m high which lay behind the Mount Inn, and to the east, where the Community and Health centres now lie, was an oval bailey 60m long by 50m wide. Streams to the south and east of the town and castle probably filled wet moats.

LLYSLUN MOTTE

SJ 033101

Owain Cyfeiliog gave this castle to Maredudd, the exiled brother of Gruffudd ap Cynan of Gwynedd in the 1170s. A natural hillock has been scarped into a tiny motte rising 3m above the ditch dividing it from a bailey platform 15m long by 12m wide.

LUGGY MOAT

SO 199022

The Luggy Brook has cut a cliff into the north side of the 9m high mound showing that it is composed of layers of rubble levelled with spreads of clay. Because of damage on the south side the summit now has a rectangular shape 16m long by 10m wide. To the east slight scarps delineate a bailey platform 54m north-south by 45m wide.

MANAFAN MOTTE

SJ 114022

The farm probably lies on the site of the bailey of the damaged 9m high mound to the NE with a summit 9m in diameter.

MATHRAFAL CASTLE

SJ 131107

Mathrafal was an original capital of the Princes of Powys, ranking alongside Aberffraw and Dinefwr as one of the three royal seats of Wales. The fort on the hill 1km NW was perhaps the original seat, and the ramparts and ditches enclosing a square of about 100m upon flat ground beside the west bank of the Banwy may be of the 10th or 11th century. The motte in the east corner and the small bailey in front of it were built either by Owain Cyfeiliog c1170 or Robert de Vieuxpont on behalf of King John in 1212 after Gwenwynwyn, son of Owain, had transferred his chief seat to Welshpool. The castle was destroyed the same year by Llywelyn Fawr. Parts of a retaining wall have been noted on the side of the bailey adjoining the river.

MIN-Y-LLYN MOTTE

SJ 210010

Beside a farm probably set on the site of a bailey is an overgrown motte rising 9m to an oval summit 18m by 15m across. Probably this castle was built in the 1080s by Roger Corbet of Caus Castle.

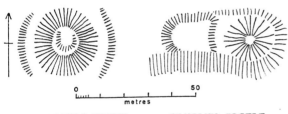

0   50
metres

MOEL FROEHAS MOTTE   LLYSLUN CASTLE

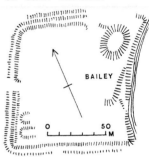

BAILEY

0   50
M

PLAN OF MATHRAFAL CASTLE

Mathrafal Motte

MOEL FROEHAS MOTTE

Two sections of ditch isolate a motte 6m high with a top 10m across from the rest of a high ridge above the Banwy with steep falls on each side except to the east where there are traces of a bailey.

MONTGOMERY CASTLE

SO 221967

The young Henry III came with his army to Montgomery in the autumn of 1223 and began work on a new castle on a high rock 2km south of Hen Domen. By November wooden buildings had been put up and Forest of Dean miners were cutting ditches through the rock. About £2,000 was spent on clearing a field of fire, providing a garrison, and walling the inner ward in stone in 1224-6. In April 1228 the King granted the castle to his Justiciar, Hubert de Burgh, Earl of Essex. It withstood attacks by Llywelyn Fawr during the summers of 1228 and 1231, although the town growing up below the castle was burnt on the latter occasion. Work on an outer court towards the Cedewain road was in hand in 1229. Hubert de Burgh fell from grace in 1232 and the castle was back in royal hands in 1233 when the main tower was roofed in lead. John le Strange was custodian in 1240.

In 1248-51 a new drawbridge, stable, and road up to the castle were provided, the middle ward gatehouse was under construction in 1251, and then £150 was spent on replacing the middle ward timber palisade with a stone wall. Henry III was at Montgomery in 1267, signing there a treaty with Llywelyn ap Gruffudd which acknowledged the latter as Prince of Wales.

Edward I had the town walled in stone in 1279-80 as part of his contest with Llywelyn ap Gruffudd, and in the 1280s over £100 was spent on providing the castle with a new hall, chamber, kitchen, bakehouse, and granary. Montgomery formed part of the dowry of Margaret, Edward's new Queen, in 1299, but was transferred to the Prince of Wales in 1301. It was granted to Edward II's widow Queen Isabella in 1327 and in 1330 was given to her lover Roger Mortimer, Earl of March. He was executed by Edward III the same year and the castle lay neglected and ruinous until granted in 1359 to Roger's grandson and namesake, who became 2nd Earl of March. He rebuilt the Well Tower and repaired the walls of the middle ward.

The castle was little used by the later Earls of March and was left to decay until Rowland Lee, Bishop of Coventry and Lichfield, was made President of the Council of the Marches of Wales in 1534. He regarded Montgomery Castle as second only in importance to his headquarters at Ludlow Castle. He renovated the buildings and the military stores, and the 100 men at work at the castle during the summer of 1538 were probably erecting the ranges of lodgings whose foundations can be seen around three sides of the middle ward.

The Herbert family were associated with Montgomery Castle as early as 1526 when Sir Richard Herbert was custodian for Henry VIII. During Elizabeth I's reign the family had a house called Blackhall in or near the town and a survey of 1593 shows the castle standing empty and decayed. In 1622 Sir Edward Herbert, created Lord Herbert of Chirbury in 1629, began to build a splendid new timber framed house in the middle ward. He yielded the castle to a Parliamentary force led by Sir Hugh Myddelton in September 1644 on condition that the building and contents were spared. However, Lord Herbert died in 1648 and as his successor Richard was an active Royalist it was ordered in 1649 that both the new house and the old castle should be demolished. Portions of the buildings, probably the upper part of the gatehouse, are said to have fallen in the early 19th century. By the 1960s, when the Earl of Powis handed the site over to Ministry of Works and excavations were begun, only two fragments stood above the mound of debris which covered most of the walls and ditches.

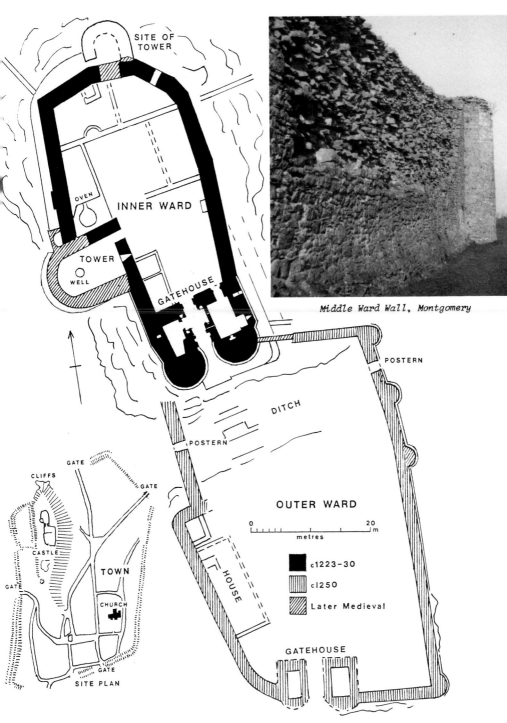

SITE OF TOWER

INNER WARD

OVEN

TOWER

WELL

GATEHOUSE

Middle Ward Wall, Montgomery

POSTERN

DITCH

POSTERN

OUTER WARD

0   20
metres   m

■ c1223–30
▦ c1250
▧ Later Medieval

HOUSE

GATEHOUSE

GATE
CLIFFS
GATE
CASTLE
TOWN
GATE
CHURCH
GATE
SITE PLAN

PLAN OF MONTGOMERY CASTLE

35

Inner Gatehouse, Montgomery Castle

The castle comprised an inner ward, a middle ward to the south, and a larger outer enclosure beyond that which probably had timber defences only and which now contains a farm. The middle ward is 60m long with a maximum width of 37m. It was defended by ditches to the south and west and had a wall 2m thick with a small round SE corner turret, and other turrets at the NE corner flanking a postern which opened out of the inner ward ditch. On the south was the gatehouse with a passage flanked by rectangular chambers with rounded fronts towards the field. Most of the wall is reduced to foundations and was perhaps lowered in the 1620s when the new Herbert mansion was built within. More survives on the east where the ground slope made a greater height of wall necessary. The space behind this wall was filled in by Bishop Lee to level the court for building upon but is now cleared out again. Traces of lodgings survive on the west side.

Two solid half-round towers 7m in diameter flank the outer part of a passage through a gatehouse 18m wide which leads to the court 39m long by 22.5m wide of the inner ward. The passageway was closed with a portcullis and two sets of doors and had two recesses with cupboards, possibly for housing lamps. The room east of the passage was for the porter or guard. That to the west was originally a dark prison only entered by a trap-door from above. A doorway was broken through from the west recess later. Only the west wall now remains of the upper levels. The hall above was reached by a timber stair from the court and according to the 1593 survey had a timber chapel set on posts built against the north side. Above were two further storeys each containing one large room with a latrine in a sidewall. A gallery connected the gatehouse apartments with chambers within the Well Tower, a big D-shaped structure 15m long by 12m wide with a well in the lowest room. Percolating water was probably the cause of continuing structural problems and most of what remains of the tower outer walls are of c1360. In 1593 the second storey room was a dining chamber. The kitchen north of the tower, and the offices and lodgings on the north and east sides of the ward, probably of the 1280s, are represented only by foundations. A D-shaped north tower was dismantled in the 1280s or 1360s and only the base still remains. East of it was a postern leading to the northern outworks.

Sections of the rampart and ditch around the town of Montgomery
survive on the west and east sides. Part of a round tower remains
near the Cottage Inn on the north side and excavations revealed the
base of another at the SW corner. Leland describes the stone walls
and the Cedewain Gate on the west, the Ceri Gate on the south, the
Chirbury Gate on the NE, and Arthur's Gate on the north as decayed
in the 1530s. Townsfolk no doubt removed stones for their houses.

NANTCRIBBA CASTLE   SJ 237014

Modern quarrying has dramatically increased the extent of natural
cliffs on the east side of a wooded hill beside Offa's Dyke. Around
the hill is a ditch, still partly water filled, possibly a relic of
a Dark Age settlement. On the overgrown summit of the hill are the
last traces of a stone wall around a court about 39m by 33m having
round towers at the west and south corners. Probably this was the
castle of Gwyddgrwg begun c1260 by Thomas Corbet of Caus Castle,
and destroyed in 1263 by Gruffudd ap Gwenwynwyn.

NEWTOWN MOTTE   SO 106915

In 1279 Cedewain was granted to Roger Mortimer and in 1280 he was
granted a charter for a weekly market which seems to have been at
Newtown, which lies within a bend of the Severn. Probably the weak
south side was then provided with a rampart and ditch, and a mound
rising 5m above a wide ditch to a summit 39m across was provided
in the middle of this side. Possibly an outer enclosure extended
westward from it to the river. The base of a small stone building on
the summit found in 1910 may have dated from 1641 when the mound
was refortified by Sir John Price. By then half the mound had been
levelled and he dug a new ditch along the resulting straight side.

NEUADD COCH MOTTE   SO 079878

Hidden in woodland is a promontory above a tributary of the Mochdre
Brook which is scarped into a motte 7m high with a top 15m long.

OLD HALL CAMP   SO 207897

On a spur high up to the south of Sarn is a ringwork thought to be
the site of a castle begun in 1228 by Hubert de Burgh in an attempt
to establish an English domination of Kerry Woods. It was called
'Hubert's Folly' when after a few weeks work it was left incomplete,
and in the 16th century the site was called Castell Machaethlon.
It has a maximum width of 45m with north and south sides curving
round to meet at right angles 60m apart at the east and west, the
entrance being at the latter. The ditch is quite formidable on the
weak SW side where there is a rampart but it was probably left much
shallower than intended on the stronger northern sides.

PEN-Y-CASTELL MOTTE   SN 954844

A ringwork 24m across rises 5m on the south but only 3m above the
ploughed out bailey 60m across to the north.

PLAS-YN-DINAS   SJ 218189

A low shelf of land above a loop of the River Vyrnwy has been made
into a defensive enclosure measuring about 125m by 105m. Possibly of
Dark Age origin, this site was still in use as late as the middle
third of the 14th century when it was held by Thomas ap Rhodri from
John de Charlton, Lord of Powis.

POWIS CASTLE

In the inner ward of Powis Castle, which is also known as Castell Coch (Red Castle) from the colour of the sandstone of which it is built, the lower parts of a square keep and separate hall block are detectable under all the later building work. Although these might normally be regarded as work of c1200 there are reasons for believing that the chief seat of the Princes of Powys remained at the motte and bailey site by the town of Welshpool until destruction by Llywelyn ap Gruffudd in 1274 because Gruffudd ap Gwenwynwyn had sided with the English. So the keep and hall block were probably began after Gruffudd was restored as ruler of Powys by Edward I of England, and continued after 1286 by his son Owain who took the English type surname of la Pole (the original name of Welshpool). Quite how the 4.5m high motte with a summit diameter of 17m lying on the shelf of land west of Powis Castle fits into the story is uncertain. Perhaps it served as an outwork of Welshpool Castle.

After Owain died in 1309 the castle passed under English law to his daughter Hawys who married John de Charlton. However under Welsh law her uncle Gruffudd claimed the castle and he besieged her within it unsuccessfully in 1312. Edward, fifth Lord Charlton, was blockaded in the castle by his own tenants in support of Glyndwr in 1403 and sought assistance from Henry IV. When Edward died in 1421 his estates were divided between his daughters. The inner ward of Powis Castle became the residence of Joan and her husband John de Grey and was kept in repair, a substantial gateway tower being added at the north end. Meanwhile the outer ward passed eventually to the Suttons, Lords of Dudley Castle in Staffordshire, who left (according to Leland) their part of Powis Castle to decay.

The castle was re-united with one family in the 16th century and in 1587 was purchased from Grey descendants by Sir Edward Herbert. He immediately began improving the accommodation at the castle and the Long Gallery and numerous windows in the outer walls are relics of this campaign while the NW range in the outer ward is probably his replacement or remodelling of a late medieval structure. His son William was created Lord Powis by Charles I in 1629, and Powis Castle was a Royalist stronghold in the Civil War until on the 2nd October 1644 Sir Thomas Myddelton captured it in a surprise night attack in which his master gunner John Arundell blew up the outer gate. The building was then left in ruins until the Restoration.

Rebuilding and remodelling began in the 1660s when a new state bedroom was installed for the 3rd Lord Powis, created an Earl in 1674 and a Marquis in 1685. The work continued under William III's nephew William Van Zuylesteyne, Earl of Rochford, who possessed the castle while the Catholic 1st and 2nd Marquis were in exile after the deposition of James II in 1688. The 2nd Marquis returned only in 1722. When the 3rd Marquis died in 1748 Powis went to an heiress who married Henry Herbert for whom George II revived the Earldom. Their daughter Henrietta married Edward Clive for whom the Powis Earldom was revived again in 1804. Part of the Clive fortune was spent on another remodelling of Powis Castle in 1815-8 to designs by Sir Robert Smirke. The 4th Earl of the new creation carried out further works early in the 20th century. His sons died in the two World Wars and when he died in 1952 the castle was given to the National Trust, although it remains a home of George Herbert, 7th Earl, who is descended from a cousin of the 4th Earl.

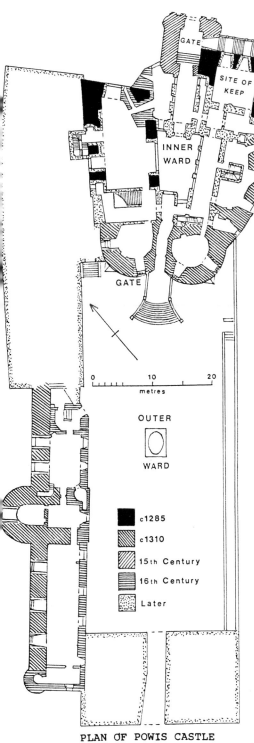

GATE

SITE OF
KEEP

INNER
WARD

GATE

```
0          10          20
|  |  |  |  |  |  |  |  |  |
         metres
```

OUTER

WARD

- ■ c1285
- ▨ c1310
- ▧ 15th Century
- ▤ 16th Century
- ░ Later

PLAN OF POWIS CASTLE

Outer Ward, Powis Castle

Powis Castle from the South

The inner ward has only a tiny central court 9m long by 7m wide within which was formerly a very deep well. The court is reached by a narrow canted passageway with two portcullis grooves. The outer arch and the massive round towers nearly 12m in diameter flanking it are of c1300-20 but the three storeys of rooms in each tower have mullion and transom windows and other features of the 1590s. The thick walled block on the NW side of the court now containing the library and Blue Drawing Room above the dining room is likely to be late 13th century work although all the features are of many dates from the late 16th century onwards. The east tower added by the Greys contained two upper living rooms above a lierne-vaulted gateway until Smirk added a fourth storey. The lower parts of the round corner turrets are original. At one time this gateway, now closed, formed the principal entrance to the castle. It adjoins a late 13th century tower roughly 13m square which formed a keep. However, the lowest storey is much altered, and the upper storeys were entirely rebuilt with thinner walling in the 1590s when part of one room became the NE end of the Long Gallery occupying the SE range second storey. This range has 16th century windows through the medieval curtain but is otherwise mostly of later centuries.

The outer ward is 30m wide and extends for 68m to the SW. The SE side is closed by a modern low level wall-walk probably on the footings of a medieval curtain. Original walling 2.8m thick remains to a great height on the NW side together with a D-shaped tower 9m in diameter. The range containing the shop and tea-room set against this wall may have 15th and 16th century masonry but was altered in the 1770s to create a narrow ballroom, south of which is a room now containing the Clive Museum. The SW range contains stables and a coach house flanking the outer gateway passage. Excavations in 1984 by the south corner revealed part of the base of a round tower which flanked the medieval gateway blown up in the attack of 1644.

Powis Castle

40

Motte near Powis Castle

RHOS DDIARBED CASTLE

SO 046905

This impressive earthwork was probably built by Roger de Montgomery in the 1080s. It is a classic motte and bailey layout on a level site which was perhaps once marshy and the ditches were probably water filled. The 9m high motte with a summit 15m across stands at the south end of an oval bailey extending 55m from the motte ditch to the entrance gap in the 4m high rampart at the north end. It is about 55m in width. A farmhouse stands within the much larger but more feebly defended rectangular outer bailey to the north.

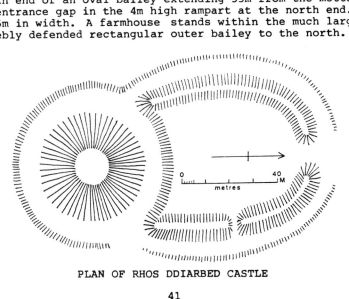

PLAN OF RHOS DDIARBED CASTLE

41

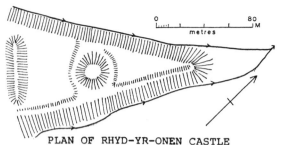

PLAN OF RHYD-YR-ONEN CASTLE

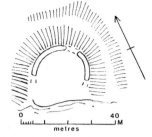

PLAN OF SYMON'S CASTLE

RHYD-YR-ONEN CASTLE   SN 923823

A motte 6m high with a summit 15m across lies across a promontory sloping from south to north where two streams far below converge. There is a small enclosure on the tip of the promontory and a much bigger one 65m wide extending 55m from the motte ditch to a high rampart on the south. Because of the slope the rampart, which has an entrance gap on the east, lies higher than the motte summit.

RHYSNANT MOTTE   SJ 256175

A very mutilated ringwork lies in wood above Rhysnant Hall.

SYMON'S CASTLE   SO 285933

A motte 4m high created by cutting a ditch through rock backs onto a cliff which has been dramatically increased in height by modern quarrying. Excavations in the 1980s revealed that the stone from the ditch was used to build a shell wall about 1.8m thick around a court 21m in diameter of which the footings still remain.

Symon's Castle

Welshpool
Motte

TAFOLWERN CASTLE   SH 891026

The low-lying motte between the Afon Twymyn and Afon Rhiw Saeson
(which may have been dammed to form moats) was probably built by
Owain Cyfeiliog, who was granted Cyfeiliog commote in 1149 by his
uncle Madog ap Maredudd. When the latter died in 1160 his relatives
quarrelled among themselves and in the confusion Cyfeiliog was taken
over by Owain Gwynedd. However, the castle, which formed the chief
seat of the commote, was captured in 1162 by Hywell ap Ieuaf, Lord
of Arwystli. Owain raided Arwystli, defeated Hywell, and rebuilt
Talfolwern Castle. By 1165 he had returned it to Owain Cyfeiliog,
but the latter was expelled from all his lands when he renewed his
former allegiance to the Normans. The castle was briefly held by
Rhys ap Gruffudd but was recaptured by Owain Cyfeiliog with Norman
help. It was occupied by Owain's son Gwenwynwyn in the later 12th
century and is last mentioned when Owain's grandson Gruffudd was
isolated there in 1244 by a Welsh army because of his support for
Henry III, and John le Strange wrote to the King urging his help.

TOMEN CEFN COCH MOTTE   SJ 105263

A mound rising 6m to a summit 11m across with traces of a ditch on
the west side lies on a commanding site above the Tanat Valley.

TOMEN MADOC MOTTE   SO 146908

The mound high up north of Kerry has been badly damaged by rabbits.

TOMEN-YR-ALLT MOTTE   SJ 126211

A now overgrown hilltop above the Nant Fyllon 2km from Llanfyllin
has been scarped into a motte 15m high with a top 10m across with
a 3m deep ditch with a counterscarp and a large bailey to the SE.
This is likely to have been the castle of Boyddon captured in 1257
by Llywelyn ap Gruffudd from Gruffudd ap Gwenwynwyn when the latter
sided with Henry III of England.

WELSHPOOL CASTLE   ST 230074

The earthwork known as Domen Castell near to Welshpool Station may
be the castle built in 1111 by Cadwgan ap Bleddyn, newly instated
as ruler of Powys. Probably it was this castle that was captured by
the English in the 1190s and soon recaptured by Gwenwynwyn. It was
still mostly a wooden structure in 1274 when Gruffudd ap Gwenwynwyn
plotted against Llywelyn ap Gruffudd and was deposed and his seat
at Pool captured and destroyed. The rampart of the oval bailey 60m
by 46m has been greatly remodelled for the use of spectators of a
bowling green created within it. On the south side is an overgrown
motte rising 5m to a summit 9m in diameter.

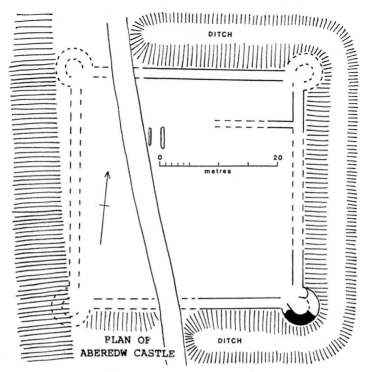

DITCH

0   20
metres

PLAN OF
ABEREDW CASTLE

DITCH

GAZETTEER OF CASTLES IN RADNORSHIRE

ABEREDW CASTLE   SO 079473 & 076474

The castle at Aberedw visited by Llywelyn ap Gruffudd just before
he was killed in a nearby skirmish with English troops in 1282 was
probably Hen Castell, a ditched motte said to have once supported
a D-shaped tower. The better known castle-site west of the village
was fortified by Walter Hakelutel, one of Edmund Mortimer's knights,
in accordance with a licence to crenellate granted in 1285. A wall
1.8m thick of which only foundations remain surrounded a courtyard
about 36m square. Part of the inner wall of a range on the north
side can be traced. At the SE corner is the base of a round tower
6m in diameter and there are signs of similar former towers at the
northern corners. The SW corner and all of the west wall vanished
when this side was cut away for building a railway. The remaining
sides have a dry moat 9m wide and over 2m deep.

BARLAND MOTTE   SO 281618

A rectangular motte rising 3m to a summit 11m long by 6m wide lies
above a south facing slope. There was perhaps a bailey to the south.

BLEDDFA CASTLE   SO 209682

The very overgrown low motte and small bailey lie SE of the church,
beside a stream. In 1195 Hugh de Say was licensed to refortify the
castle and the square tower of which slight traces remain on top of
the motte was probably built not long after, although Hugh himself
was killed at the battle of Radnor in the same year. The castle was
destroyed in 1262 after being captured by Llywelyn ap Gruffudd from
the Mortimers. Probably materials from it were used in c1300-40 to
build the church tower, itself destroyed by the Welsh in c1403.

Aberedw Castle

BOUGHROOD CASTLE   SO 132391

The castle was probably built by a younger brother of Cadwallon, Lord of Maelienydd, Einion Clyd, who was murdered in 1140, or his son Walter Fychan to whom Boughrood was eventually restored by the Bishop of Hereford. It was later held by the Gamage family and then the Walshes. A stone tower at Boughrood is recorded in 1205 and an excavation was carried out on the mound beside Castle Farm in 1966 expecting to reveal the base of a square tower keep. However, only fragments of mortar and 13th century pottery were found, all stones having been robbed, perhaps in 1800 when Francis Foulke erected a mansion on or near the castle site.

BURFA MOTTE   SO 275611

The 4m high mound has a D-shaped summit 17m long by 13m wide as a result of the collapse or erosion of the eastern side.

CASTELL CAEMARDY   SO 035530

A small motte lies on a hill 2km north of Builth Wells.

CASTELL CRUGERYDD   SO 158593

On a commanding spur west of the A44 is a D-shaped bailey platform 47m in diameter by 28m wide rising up to 2m above the surrounding ditch. A motte with its own ditch lies on the straight west side. It rises 4m to a summit 8m in diameter. This castle was visited by Giraldus Cambrensis on his tour of Wales in 1188. It is likely to derive its name from the herald-bard Llywelyn Crug Eryr who lived timber buildings here in c1300.

CASTELL FOEL ALT   SO 258676

In a flat meadow beside the River Lugg below Pilleth Church are the last remnants of a small and worn down motte.

Castell Gemaron

CASTELL GEMARON

SO 153703

Alternatively known as Cymaron or Cwm Aran, this castle continued to serve the Mortimers as a manorial seat until the end of the 13th century. It is first mentioned in 1144 when it was rebuilt, having probably been destroyed by the Welsh. The castle was repaired in 1179 and rebuilt in 1195, but fell to Llywelyn Fawr in 1202. A farmhouse lies within the eastern half of a quadrangular bailey 60m long by 50m wide with a steep fall to the River Aran on the east, and a rampart and ditch on the other sides. On the south is a big but rather shapeless motte without a flat summit and on the SW is a high counterscarp bank helping to shield the bailey from higher ground beyond. Further west is a tributary stream.

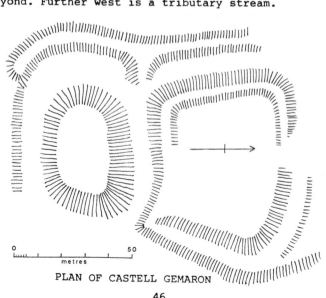

PLAN OF CASTELL GEMARON

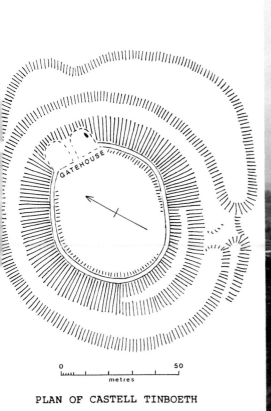

PLAN OF CASTELL TINBOETH

Castell Tinboeth

CASTELL TINBOETH

SO 090755

Also known as Castell Dinbaud, after Maud, widow of Roger Mortimer, this castle lies at 400m on a commanding hill high above the River Irthon and a tributary to the south. It comprises a platform about 50m in diameter surrounded by a rock-cut ditch as much as 9m deep in places with a counterscarp that on the east side extends into an elliptical outer platform 16m wide. The original buildings, perhaps of wood, were destroyed by Llywelyn ap Gruffudd in 1260, and a new stone curtain of which only buried footings now survive was built in c1275-82. On the NE side are several fallen fragments and just one small standing fragment of a gatehouse of uncertain shape but there are no signs of any other towers or internal buildings. The castle was garrisoned against the Welsh in 1282 and was taken from the Mortimers by Edward II in 1322. It was little used afterwards.

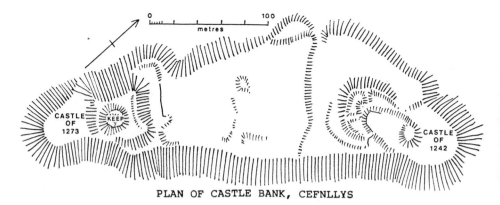

PLAN OF CASTLE BANK, CEFNLLYS

CASTLE NIMBLE
SO 247594

Beside a stream in a valley below Old Radnor church are a very low motte 18m in diameter and a bailey about 25m square. Presumably a combination of wet moats and marshland made the site defensible.

CEFNLLYS CASTLE
SO 088614 & 092630

The D-shaped motte rising 5m to a dished summit 18m in diameter beside a ford across the River Ithon 1.5km NNE of the church might be the castle built by Ralph Mortimer, who succeeded his father Roger before 1086 and is last mentioned in 1104. Before long a new castle seems to have been erected at the NE end of the four acre hilltop known as Castle Bank which is almost surrounded by a wide and deep bend of the Ithon within which lies the church, and which was probably occupied in the Iron Age. It was probably this castle which was refortified by Hugh Mortimer in 1144. Certainly the new stone defences begun in c1242 by Ralph Mortimer were on this site. They were probably nearly complete by 1246, when he died, leaving only a daughter. His castle appears to have comprised a round keep with an oval bailey 50m long by 40m wide to the west with an outer bailey of similar size at a lower level to the east.

In November 1262 the Welsh of Maelienydd revolted against the Mortimers. At Cefnllys they killed the castle porters, captured the constable, and destroyed the castle. Roger Mortimer and Humphrey de Bohun brought a force to the district and camped in the ruins but Llywelyn ap Gruffudd besieged them there and they were obliged to accept the offer of a free passage back to their territories east of Offa's Dyke. The Treaty of Montgomery made in 1267 allowed Roger Mortimer to refortify the site. The Prince and baron disagreed on the interpretation of this and Llywelyn complained to Edward I when in 1273-4 a new castle was built at Cefnllys instead of rebuilding the older structure of the 1240s. The new castle was evidently the building which stood at the more cramped SW tip of the long narrow triangular hilltop. There the ground falls away very steeply all round except to the NE where a deep moat was cut through the rock. The new building comprised a large circular or octagonal tower keep standing in the middle of a courtyard about 35m square with towers at the corners, that to the east containing the entrance. To the SW was an outer court of similar size at a lower level. The older castle 180m away was no doubt levelled to the ground and material from it re-used. Edmund Mortimer garrisoned the new castle against Llywelyn in 1282 with 8 horsemen and 20 infantrymen. The market he granted to the men of Maelienydd in 1297 was probably to be held on the hilltop beside the new castle, and at his death in 1304 the town had 25 burgesses suggesting a total population of over 100.

Castle Bank, Cefnllys

Roger Mortimer was obliged to surrender his estates to Edward II in 1322 because of his part in Thomas of Lancaster's rebellion. Maelienydd was granted to the Earl of Kent along with the castle of Cefnllys, now the capital of the district after the demise of Gemaron Castle. Mortimer only recovered Cefnllys after he deposed Edward in 1326. Soon after his execution by the young Edward III in 1330 Maelienydd and other confiscated estates were granted to his son Edmund, who died in 1331 leaving Cefnllys to his widow. On her death in 1356 her son Roger repaired the barn, prison, the hall steps, and the roof of the keep.

Edmund Mortimer was a minor during Owain Glyndwr's rebellion and Cefnllys was thus in royal custody. Hugh Burnell was there in charge of a garrison of 12 spearmen and thirty archers. In 1403 the Bishop and Sheriff of Worcester were ordered to supply them with 8 quarters of wheat, 1 tun of wine, 3 tuns of ale, 200 fish, and 60 quarters of oats. The area around was devastated by the Welsh but the castle appears to have remained unharmed.

The vast estates of Edmund Mortimer passed by marriage in 1432 to Richard, Duke of York. He appointed Ieuan ap Philip as constable of Cefnllys Castle. Ieuan's bard Lewis Glyn Cothi wrote a series of poems which have survived. They refer to the rebuilding of the castle hall, and the eight-sided fort which is mentioned may refer to the central tower keep. Cefnllys was merged with the Crown in 1461 when Edward, Duke of York, seized the throne. The castle was granted by Henry VII to his eldest son Arthur in 1493 but probably soon afterwards was abandoned. Camden calls it a ruin in 1558, and the manorial court was transferred to the nearby farm of Neuadd.

CLYRO CASTLE   SO 214435

South of a housing estate is a natural hillock which has been made into a large mound up to 40m across on top. There is a ditch and a few buried foundations of a curtain wall and internal buildings.

Knighton Motte

COLWYN CASTLE

SO 108540

The farm on a hillock above the Edw occupies a ringwork 60m across with a ditch and counterscarp. It lies within a larger rectangular enclosure. The castle was rebuilt in 1144 after destruction by the Welsh. It has an alternative name of Maud's castle after the wife of William de Braose who rebuilt it after destruction in 1195-6. It was rebuilt in stone c1240 but all the masonry vanished long ago.

COURT EVAN GLYNNE

SO 215447

A farmhouse called Castle Kinsey occupies the bailey platform of an overgrown mound about 4m high.

DOLBEDWYN MOTTE

SO 205491

Above a bend of a tributary of the River Arrow is a tree-covered mound which has collapsed on the south side, where it is 3m high.

EVANJOBB MOTTE

SO 266625

A tiny mound lies in a field behind a farmhouse NE of the village.

HUNDRED HOUSE MOTTE

SO 116542

A well preserved motte about 5m high with trees upon it lies at the SW corner of a rectangular banked enclosure by the River Edw.

KNIGHTON CASTLES

SO 284722 & 290722

Bryn Castell, a mound rising 2.5m above a ditch 1m deep to a summit 18m in diameter beside playing fields east of the town, was perhaps the site of the original castle of c1100. Later a new motte still surviving in an overgrown state in a garden at the west end of the town was built. A bailey lay between it and the steep fall to the Wylcwm Brook. The motte is 4m high and bears walling of uncertain date and purpose. This site is mentioned in the Pipe Rolls of 1182 and again in 1191-2 when William de Braose is named in connection with building works on the site. The castle was probably allowed to be enveloped by the growing town after being destroyed in 1262 by Llywelyn ap Gruffudd. In 1260 the burgesses of the town secured a grant of murage for the construction of defences, and it appears that the settlement was regarded as defensible in 1402 when Edmund Mortimer sent 400 men from Ludlow to hold it against the Welsh. No walls survive and a rampart, stockade, and ditch may have been considered sufficient as the site is naturally quite strong and Offa's Dyke passes very closeby to the west of the town.

Knucklas Castle

KNUCKLAS CASTLE
SO 250745

On a hilltop high above the village and a tributary of the Teme are the buried footings of a curtain wall around a courtyard about 30m square with round corner towers. Slightly more survives of the east wall although it is defaced externally and buried internally so no thickness can be determined. The remainder of the hilltop seems to have formed a D-shaped outer court defended by a palisade. On the south is a deep pit. The castle is said to have been built by Hugh Mortimer II in c1220-30, and was destroyed by Llywelyn ap Gruffudd in 1262. It is uncertain whether the remains are of before or after that date but it is possible it was never rebuilt. It is not among the castles of Roger Mortimer seized by Edward II in 1322 nor the strongholds fortified against Owain Glyndwr in 1403. In the 1480s Philip ap Howel, who helped Henry VII defeat Richard III, held the manor but there is no evidence that he occupied or used the castle.

LLANBEDR MOTTE
SO 126459

A tree-clad mound 5m high lies by a track above Bach Howey brook.

NEW RADNOR CASTLE

The historical relationship between the castle of New Radnor, the moated site south of Old Radnor Church, and Castle Nimble in the valley north of Old Radnor is uncertain, but it is likely that all the early references to Radnor mean New Radnor and that Philip de Braose had a castle on this fine defensive site by c1095. It was destroyed by the Welsh in 1196 after they won a battle nearby, and was destroyed again by them in 1216, 1231, and 1262. It was rebuilt by Edward Mortimer and was garrisoned against the Welsh in 1282. The discovery in 1845, when foundation trenches were dug for the new church, of many headless skeletons and a separate pile of skulls shows fairly clearly what happened to the garrison of 60 men after Owain Glyndwr's forces captured the castle in 1402. The castle was subsequently left to decay and in 1535 Bishop Roland Lee reported to Thomas Cromwell that the only part worth repairing was that in use as the county prison. This was evidently within the gatehouse as Leland refers specifically to that part as recently repaired.

The Earls of Pembroke were nominal constables of Radnor Castle in James I's reign, and Lord Powis in 1631. The castle was able to briefly accommodate Prince Charles in 1642 but soon afterwards was captured and dismantled by Parliamentary forces. Small cannon balls used in the siege were discovered in the 1780s and one larger ball was embedded in a wall. In 1815 Thomas Rees recorded the castle as being nearly square with massive square towers at the north, east, and NW corners, with two smaller round towers towards the town but it is likely that he was describing what appears on Speed's map of 1610 rather than observed remains. Pointed arches and foundations were revealed by digging in 1773, 1818, and 1864, the well being discovered on the latter occasion. There were still standing walls in 1840. Only earthworks now survive. The oval inner ward 58m long by 35m wide overlooks a steep drop to the High Street on the south and to the Dingle Brook on the east. To the north and west it is separated from a large but weakly defended bailey 150m long by 60m wide by a formidable system of two wide and deep dry ditches.

New Radnor Castle earthworks

Town Rampart, New Radnor

Roger Mortimer obtained a murage grant for walling in the town in 1257 and further grants were made in 1280, 1283, and 1290. from the SW corner of the castle bailey a rampart still survives almost to the Summergil Brook, which probably fed a partially wet moat, and then onto the site of the South Gate. South of the site of the West Gate shale walling is visible in the bank. Less survives of the eastern section of the defences, where there was a third gate, and the NE section, with a fourth gate near the Dingle Brook. The defences were probably never restored after the destruction wrought in 1403 from which the town never recovered. It only attained the status of county town in 1536 because of the castle being used as a prison, and soon lost that status to more prosperous Presteigne.

NORTON MOTTE   SO 305673

A motte and bailey castle lies beside the village which is set upon a hillock above a tributary of the River Lugg. Norton was among the Mortimer castles captured in the 1260s by Llywelyn ap Gruffudd.

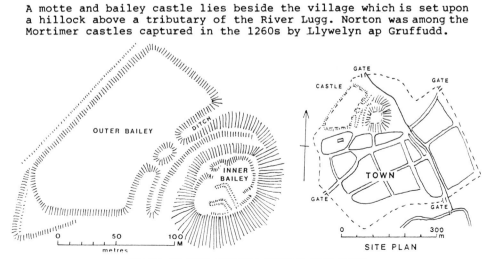

PLANS OF NEW RADNOR CASTLE AND TOWN

Pain's Castle earthworks

PAIN'S CASTLE

SO 166462

This castle is named after its builder Pain Fitz-John, who died in c1136. His descendants took the surname Fitz-Payn. In the 1190s the castle was held by William de Braose. He had Talhaiarn, cousin of Gwenwynwyn, Prince of Powys, dragged through Brecon tied to a horse and then beheaded and Gwenwynwyn sought revenge by besieging Pain's Castle. De Braose enlisted the help of other Welsh lords hostile to the Lord of Powys, who was defeated, losing 3,700 men. After being destroyed by the Welsh the castle was rebuilt in stone by Henry III in 1251 with a round tower keep on the motte and a curtain with an east gatehouse and several towers. It was damaged by the Welsh in 1265 but was restored and was garrisoned by the Earl of Warwick in 1401 against Owain Glyndwr. Only earthworks remain, comprising a 9m high motte with a summit 22m long, a bailey 60m wide by 45m long to the north, and a deep surrounding ditch with a counterscarp.

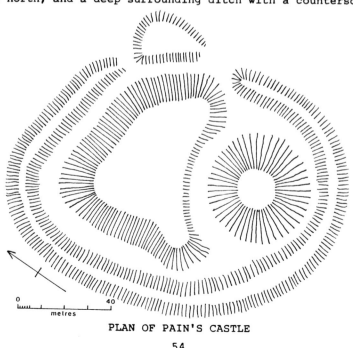

```
0          40
|‒‒‒‒|‒‒‒‒‒|
   metres
```

PLAN OF PAIN'S CASTLE

54

PENARTH MOTTE

On a spur above the River Edw is a mound rising 5m to a dished top 15m long by 13m wide. There are ditches 1m deep to the NE and SW.

RHAYADER CASTLE

SN 968680

The castle built by Rhys ap Gruffudd in 1177 was burnt in 1195. It was rebuilt and despite later destructions probably remained in use until the 14th century. It was protected on the NW and SW by a bend of the River Wye. On the other two sides was a rock-cut ditch with a narrow entrance causeway left at the NE corner. Within the ditch was a spring. Most of the ditch was later filled in with rubbish.

TOMEN BEDURGE MOTTE

SO 101695

A motte and bailey lie on a hill above the west side of the Ithon.

TOMEN MOTTE

SO 173589

A tiny mound lies on a spur above a stream near Castell Crugerydd.

A GLOSSARY OF TERMS

Bailey	- An enclosure defended by palisades, walls, or moats.
Barbican	- Porch, tower, or small court in front of a gateway.
Batter	- An inward inclination of a wall face.
Battlement	- A parapet with crenellations.
Crenels	- Indentations between the merlons on a parapet.
Curtain Walls	- High stone walls around a castle bailey or ward.
Jamb	- The side of a doorway, window, or other opening.
Keep	- A building or a small court acting as a citadel.
Light	- A compartment of a window.
Loop	- A narrow opening for light or for missile discharge.
Moat	- A ditch, wet or dry, around an enclosure or bailey.
Motte	- Mound, usually artificial, built to support a keep.
Mullion	- A vertical member dividing the lights of a window.
Parapet	- A wall for protection at any sudden drop.
Plinth	- The battered or stepped projecting base of a wall.
Ringwork	- A small enclosure defended by a high rampart.
Roll Moulding	- Moulding of semi-circular or D-shaped section.
Shell Keep	- Small stone walled enclosure on top of a motte.
Solar	- Castle owner's living room, often also his bedroom.
Transom	- Horizontal member dividing top & bottom window lights.
Wall Walk	- A walkway on a wall top, protected by a parapet.
Ward	- More confined version of a bailey, with stone walls.

FURTHER READING

The Towns of Medieval Wales, Ian Soulsby, 1983
Castles of The Welsh Princes, Paul R. Davis, 1988
Powys (Buildings of Wales Series), Richard Haslam, 1979
Guides to the castles of Powis, Montgomery, and Tretower
A History of The County of Brecknock, 4 vols, Theophilus Jones 1909
Periodicals: Brycheiniog, Montgomeryshire Collections, Radnorshire Society Transactions, Medieval Archeology, Archeologia Cambrensis.

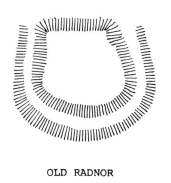

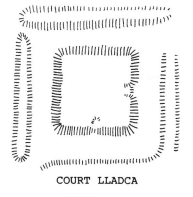

OLD RADNOR   COURT LLADCA   TALACHDDU

PLANS OF MOATED SITES

MOATED SITES IN MID WALES

Several moated sites lie either side of the A470 Brecon-Hay road. That at SO 076321 has a dry shallow ditch 8m wide around a platform 32m long by 24m wide. The platform 29m square at 100336 had a much wider moat fed by the Dulas Brook, with outer banks. The sites at 113346, 119326, and 150365 were of similar size, the latter being much damaged. The larger moat which once enclosed a rectory at 143348 beside Bronllys church is filled in on the east and NE but still contains water on the south side.

In Montgomeryshire there is a large quadrangular enclosure with signs of an outer court at SJ 277129, beside Old Mills Farm. There are smaller quadrangular sites at SO 285958, near Old Church Stoke, SO 094983, below the drive to Gregynog House, SJ 222113, by a house at Guilsfield, and another possible former rectory site at Meifod, at SJ 222113, north of the church, where two streams converge.

Radnorshire has a quadrangular moat at SO 225445, near Hay, and a larger example possibly of Dark Age origin at SO 026532, beside Builth Road Station. The more rounded platform at SO 250590 beside Old Radnor Church has a formidable ditch but is commanded by higher ground to the south. Perhaps it is another former rectory site.

Moat at Old Radnor